Ayodhya: The Dark Night

Ayodhya: The Dark Night

The Secret History of Rama's Appearance in Babri Masjid

Krishna Jha and Dhirendra K. Jha

HarperCollins *Publishers* India
a joint venture with

New Delhi

First published in India in 2012 by
HarperCollins *Publishers* India
a joint venture with
The India Today Group

ISBN: 978-93-5029-600-4

2 4 6 8 10 9 7 5 3 1

HarperCollins *Publishers*
A-53, Sector 57, Noida, Uttar Pradesh 201301, India
77-85 Fulham Palace Road, London W6 8JB, United Kingdom
Hazelton Lanes, 55 Avenue Road, Suite 2900, Toronto, Ontario M5R 3L2
and 1995 Markham Road, Scarborough, Ontario M1B 5M8, Canada
25 Ryde Road, Pymble, Sydney, NSW 2073, Australia
31 View Road, Glenfield, Auckland 10, New Zealand
10 East 53rd Street, New York NY 10022, USA

Typeset in Calisto MT 10/13
InoSoft Systems Noida

Printed and bound at
Thomson Press (India) Ltd.

Contents

Introduction

The night was almost over. Ayodhya was still numb with sleep. Piercing through the quiet, a young sadhu, drenched in sweat, came scampering from Hanumangarhi, a fortress-like Hindu religious establishment housing over five hundred sadhus in Ayodhya. He had been sent to summon Satyendra Das to his guru, Abhiram Das, who seemed to be breathing his last. Those were the early hours of 3 December 1981, and a curtain was coming down over a few forgotten pages of history.

Dharam Das, the other disciple who stayed with Abhiram Das in his one-room tenement, the asan in Hanumangarhi, had asked for him so that they could be with their guru in his last moments. The news did not come as a shock. Satyendra Das had been almost awaiting the moment, since he had known for long that his guru was nearing the end of his journey. He had been at his bedside the whole day and the signs were not encouraging. Even when he had left Abhiram Das's asan to get a breather after hours of tending to the terminally ill, he had a premonition that his guru – the man who had led a small band of Hindus to surreptitiously plant the idol of Lord Rama in Babri Masjid on yet another December night three decades ago – might not live long. After he had come away from the bedside, unwilling but tired to the bones, Satyendra Das was restless and unable to sleep. He dreaded the moment, yet knew that someone would knock on his doors with the news any time, and when it came, he responded fast, wrapped a quilt around himself and ran out along with the young sadhu who had come to fetch him.[1]

It was very cold outside. The winter night was fading into a dense fog that smothered everything in its folds. Nothing was visible. The duo, almost running in total invisibility, knew the nooks and crannies of Ayodhya like the back of their hands. As Satyendra Das arrived at the asan, he saw Abhiram Das lying in the middle of the room on a charpoy, surrounded by a few sadhus from Hanumangarhi. No one spoke; it was very quiet. Only Dharam Das moved close to him and murmured softly that their guru had passed away minutes before he had stepped in. Slowly, as the day began to break, devotees and disciples started pouring into the room. Soon, preparations for the last rites of the deceased were begun with the help of some residents of Hanumangarhi.

The rituals for the final journey of ascetics are not the same as those for non-ascetic Hindu grihasthas, particularly in north India. Sadhus, unlike Hindu grihasthas, are rarely cremated. There are two options: either their bodies are smeared with salt and buried sitting in a meditative posture or they are dropped down a sacred river tied with a rock or sacks full of sand. The fact that sadhus who take vows of complete renunciation are not cremated symbolizes their separation from the material world. The claim goes that cremation for sadhus is superfluous since they have already burnt their attachments through ascetic initiation, opting for a life of austerities and renunciation.[2]

In Ayodhya, the normal ascetic practice has been to immerse the body of a sadhu in the Sarayu – the name given to the river only as long as it touches the shores of the town. Before and after Ayodhya, the river is known as the Ghaghara. The reason for this nomenclatural confusion lies in a particular Hindu belief. As mythology has turned Ayodhya into the birthplace of Lord Rama, the river flowing by it has also assumed the mythical name of

Sarayu – the stream that is believed to have flowed through the kingdom of Lord Rama.

Back in Hanumangarhi, by the noon of 3 December 1981, Abhiram Das's disciples and friends had completed all preparations and were ready to initiate the final rituals for the deceased. Outside the asan, the body of Abhiram Das had been placed on a platform made of bamboo in a seated posture, his face frozen into a mask of self-control, his eyes half-closed as if he were deep in meditation. A saffron piece of cloth that had the name of Lord Rama printed all over – a particular kind of cotton or silk material called ramnami – had been carefully wrapped around his body. A similar cloth covered three sides of the arch made out of split bamboo that rested on the hard bamboo platform holding the corpse. The bamboo structure – euphemistically called viman to symbolize the mythical transporter of souls to the heavenly realm – had been kept uncovered on one side to enable people to have a last glimpse of the deceased.

Slowly, a group of sadhus lifted the viman on their shoulders and climbed up the flight of stairs leading to the temple of Lord Hanuman in the centre of Hanumangarhi. At the temple, the group swelled further and as the viman was taken out of Hanumangarhi, the motley crowd accompanying it chanted, 'Ramajanmabhoomi Uddharak amar rahen (Long live the saviour of the birth place of Rama).'

Three decades back, on the morning of 23 December 1949, the First Information Report (FIR) registered by Ayodhya Police following the planting of the idol of Lord Rama in Babri Masjid on the night before had named Abhiram Das as the prime accused. He had also been tried for the crime he and his friends had committed that night, but the case had remained inconclusive. In course of time, many Hindus in Ayodhya had started calling him Ramajanmabhoomi Uddharak.

The slogan-shouting grew louder as the viman reached the entrance of Babri Masjid, where it was carefully laid down. The priests of Ramajanmabhoomi, the temple that operated inside Babri Masjid ever since the idol was planted in it, as well as those of nearby Hindu religious establishments already knew about the demise of the sadhu, and they came out and garlanded the corpse and paid their homage to the departed soul.

By and large, however, Ayodhya remained unaware of Abhiram Das's death. Though some residents looked at this funeral procession with curiosity, for the majority it was the demise of yet another old sadhu. After three decades, the historical facts associated with the developments in 1949 had slipped into obscurity. The propaganda of All India Hindu Mahasabha and Rashtriya Swayamsevak Sangh (RSS) – that the idol had never been planted and Lord Rama had manifested *himself* at *his* place of birth – had gained ground among devout Hindus by now, largely delinking Abhiram Das from what he had done in the dark hours of that fateful night. Booklets and pamphlets written by Hindu communalists during the intervening period had flooded the shops of Ayodhya and had gone a long way in reinforcing the myth of 'divine exercise'. For legal reasons, even those who had a role in that surreptitious act found it convenient to let the myth grow and capture popular imagination. The law, after all, could catch human conspiracies, but a 'divine exercise' was beyond its reach. Yet, to a small group of Hindus in Ayodhya, Abhiram Das continued to remain till his death Ramajanmabhoomi Uddharak or simply Uddharak Baba.

Whatever be the case, the lack of interest among locals could not be missed by many present in the cortège as it wound down the narrow lanes of Ayodhya and moved towards the banks of the Sarayu.[3] On the bank, where the cortège reached at around two that afternoon, those carrying the viman on their shoulders bent down to put their burden on the ground. The sadhu's body was taken out of it, bathed in the river and, after being smeared with ghee all over, was wrapped in a fresh white cloth. Two sand-filled sacks were tied to the back of the body, one beneath the shoulder and the other under the waist, which was then gently laid out in the boat that sailed off the moment Satyendra Das, Dharam Das and three other sadhus of Hanumangarhi boarded it. Within minutes, the boat reached the centre of the river, where it was no longer shallow and which had traditionally been used for such water burials. Those present on the boat performed the final rites before lifting Abhiram Das's body and casting it into the cool, calm waters of the Sarayu.

II

The indifferent response that Abhiram Das's death evoked among the local populace in 1981 was at odds with the atmosphere the town had witnessed three decades ago, during the years following Independence. At that time, many in Ayodhya, as in several other parts of the country, had seen things differently. The communal frenzy which had accompanied the partition of India had intensely brutalized the atmosphere. No less important was the role played by organizations which saw the immediate aftermath of Partition as an opportunity to derail the secular project of independent India. The conspirators associated with these organizations and the conspiracies they hatched had already resulted in major national tragedies.

One such was the gruesome murder of Mahatma Gandhi on 30 January 1948. The hands that pumped bullets into the chest of the Mahatma were that of Nathuram Godse, but, as was proved later, the assassination was part of a conspiracy hatched by top Hindu Mahasabha leaders, led by V.D. Savarkar, whose prime objectives were to snatch political initiative from the Congress and destabilize all efforts to uphold secularism in India.[4] The conspiracy to kill Gandhi could not remain hidden for long even though the trial, held immediately after the assassination, had failed to uncover its extent.

The surreptitious occupation of the Babri Masjid was an act planned by almost the same set of people about two years later – on the night of 22 December 1949. It was, in many ways, a reflection of the same brutalized atmosphere that saw Gandhi being murdered. Neither the conspirators nor their underlying objectives were different. In both instances, the conspirators belonged to the Hindu Mahasabha leadership – some of the prime movers of the planting of the idol had been the prime accused in the Gandhi murder case – and their objective this time too was to wrest the political centre stage from the Congress by provoking large-scale Hindu mobilization in the name of Lord Rama.

Yet the two incidents differed – as much in the modus operandi used by Hindu communalists as in the manner in which the government and the ruling party, the Congress, responded to them. While the Mahatma was killed in full public view in broad daylight, the Babri Masjid was converted into a temple secretly, in the dead of night. Apparently, the quick and massive government reprisal in the aftermath of Gandhi's assassination had taught the Hindu Mahasabha leaders several lessons. One was to avoid confrontation with the government so that they could extract maximum political advantage out of their act. Another was to involve a section of the Congress that was sympathetic to their cause. So when, two years later, they set out to execute the Ayodhya project, they remained extremely careful, keeping themselves in the backstage until the mosque was actually impounded and ensuring a large-scale mobilization of Hindus in the immediate aftermath without wasting any time. Though the political objective they had planned through this act of communal aggression in Ayodhya could not be achieved in the manner they had hoped for, they greatly succeeded in keeping the story of the night and the conspiracy behind it a secret, for it never came out in its entirety.

Also, while the conspiracy to kill the Mahatma was probed thoroughly by a commission set up by the Government of India albeit two decades later, no such inquiry was conducted to unmask the plot and the plotters behind the forcible conversion of the Babri Masjid into a temple. As a result, an event that so remarkably changed the political discourse in India continues to be treated as a localized crime committed spontaneously by a handful of local people led, of course, by Abhiram Das, a local sadhu. It was, however, a well-planned conspiracy involving national-, provincial- and local-level leaders of the Hindu Mahasabha undertaken with the objective of reviving the party's political fortunes that were lost in the aftermath of the Gandhi assassination.

Time has further pushed the secret story of the Hindu Mahasabha's Ayodhya strategy into obscurity, leaving only what is most apparent for public debate. The unending process of litigation which it triggered completely shifted the focus away from that fateful night and has now become the basis of communal politics in the country. Incidentally, the most crucial part of the controversy – the hidden one – remains an ignored area of research. For instance, the White Paper on the Babri Masjid–Ramajanmabhoomi dispute of the Government of India dismissed the incident of 1949 – legally the root cause of the dispute – in just one paragraph. Issued in the aftermath of the demolition of the mosque on 6 December 1992, the document does not have more to say on the incident:

> The controversy entered a new phase with the placing of idols in the disputed structure in December 1949. The premises were attached under Section 145 of the Code of Criminal Procedure. Civil suits were filed shortly thereafter. Interim orders in these civil suits restrained the parties from removing the idols or interfering with their worship. In effect, therefore, from December 1949 till December 6, 1992 the structure had not been used as a mosque.[5]

It seems impertinent to say that so little is known about the night of 22–23 December 1949 since, in a sense, almost the entire dispute over the mosque emanates from the appearance of the idol of Rama inside that structure. Nevertheless, it is true that there has been little research by contemporary or later writers to fill the gap. This missing link of history remained out of focus till the issue was politically revived and strengthened by the Vishwa Hindu Parishad (VHP) in the mid-1980s. And by then the story of the night had been taken over by the politics of communalism and the debate over the proprietorship of the disputed land.

But till Lord Rama 'manifested' *himself* inside the Babri Masjid, all moves had sought to construct the temple at Ramachabutara, an elevated platform outside the inner courtyard of the mosque. Only *after* the idols were placed inside did the demand for converting the Muslim place of worship into a temple enter the legal arena. And yet the development of that night did not attract much attention in the media when it actually took place. No major newspaper or journal of the time gave it the kind of serious coverage it deserved even though the import of the development was not at all lost on Congress leaders like Jawaharlal Nehru, Sardar Vallabhbhai Patel, Govind Ballabh Pant and Akshay Brahmachary as well as Hindu Mahasabha president N.B. Khare, its vice-president V.G. Deshpande and its all India general secretary and president of the party's UP unit Mahant Digvijai Nath.

The only journal that covered the events in detail was a local Hindi weekly in Ayodhya called *Virakta*. Its editor, Ramgopal Pandey 'Sharad', was a known Mahasabhaite. The kind of material that *Virakta* published had a pronounced Hindu communal bias, and it was hardly expected to carry objective reportage on the developments. If anything, this journal was the first to promote the theory of 'divine exercise' – though in bits and pieces – to explain the appearance of the idol of Lord Rama inside the mosque.

Later, Ramgopal Pandey 'Sharad' wrote a booklet in Hindi – *Shree Ramjanmabhoomi Ka Rakta Ranjit Itihaas* (The Blood-soaked History of the Birth Place of Lord Rama). In Ayodhya, this has remained the most popular and perhaps only available material on the subject ever since. Like *Virakta*, this booklet, too, explains the developments of that night in terms of divine intervention rather than as a communal tactic conceived and executed by the Mahasabha in collaboration with local communalists. This is what the booklet says:

> Twenty-third December 1949 was a glorious day for India. On that day, after a long gap of about four hundred years, the birth place of Lord Rama was redeemed. The way developments happened [on the night before], it can be said that Lord Rama himself redeemed his place of birth.[6]

While this theory was being used by communalists to explain the mystery of those dark hours, no serious attempt was made to explore the events of that night objectively, neither by the government nor by any institutions or individual researchers. Debunking the theory of 'divine exercise' is one thing (and there is no dearth of works in this regard), but unravelling the truth that was sought to be covered is something else.

Surely, part of the reason why the facts could not come out as and when they occurred – as happened in case of Mahatma Gandhi's assassination – had greatly to do with the power politics of the time. After the assassination of Gandhi in 1948 until the death of Sardar Vallabhbhai Patel in 1950, the Congress party was beset with an intense intra-party power struggle. Though it had witnessed factional fights earlier as well, there had always been an element of restraint under the influence of Mahatma Gandhi and the idealism of the freedom struggle. But as soon as these restraints disappeared, the fight between the two power blocs in the Congress – Hindu conservatives led by Patel and secularists led by Nehru – came out in the open.

The United Provinces, in particular, emerged as one of the main battlegrounds for these power blocs in the Congress, merely months after Gandhi's assassination. Govind Ballabh Pant, the chief minister of the province (called prime minister before adoption of the Constitution on 26 January 1950), was a staunch loyalist of Patel. His desperation to remove all those who appeared to be potential challengers to his authority in the state Congress led him to align with Hindu revivalists in Ayodhya – a move that, apart from paying him dividends, greatly emboldened Mahasabhaites and set the ground for the eventual appearance of the idols at the Babri Masjid.

With the Hindu conservative faction of the Congress, in a bid to neutralize Nehru, openly trying to outsource political strength from communal elements outside the party, and the latter endeavouring to arrest this political drift and salvage its own position, there was hardly much time, or determination, to probe the misdeeds of the

Mahasabhaites. This was even more so in the United Provinces where the government appeared to be more interested in protecting the Hindu communalists than bringing them to book.

By the time this battle was won by Nehru in late 1950, the incidents of the night of 22 December 1949 had got lost in legal thickets, and the mood of the nation had changed, with the secular fabric seemingly no longer threatened by Hindu revivalists. As the focus shifted following the promulgation of the Constitution of India on 26 January 1950, almost all the players of the Hindu Mahasabha's Ayodhya strategy either lost their relevance or, in cases where some of them managed to remain in currency, their ability to break the secular equilibrium got severely restricted and their link with the night became part of this missing link of modern India's history.

III

For all the mystery shrouding the night of 22 December 1949, one name that popped up – and remained the sole visible part of the Hindu Mahasabha's Ayodhya strategy – was that of Abhiram Das. In Ayodhya, however, not much is known about the antecedents of this sadhu. The reason for this lack of knowledge about his past life has greatly to do with the ascetic belief system. It is a convention among ascetics not to enquire about the personal life and background of a sadhu, particularly about his existence before becoming an ascetic. 'Jat na puchho sadhu ki (Do not ask the caste of an ascetic)' is the usual refrain among those who have renounced the world. It is believed that at the time of initiation into an ascetic sect and renunciant status, sadhus symbolically 'die' with regard to their previous social identity. They renounce their former life and social relationships and sever all connections with their personal history. Their lifestyle, ritual practices and belief system emphasize separation and detachment from the material world, and their religious activities and aspirations are directed towards spiritual transcendence and union with God through the practice of yoga, austerities and devotionalism.

So who was Abhiram Das? Where had he come from and how did he become a sadhu? What motivations acted upon him? And what kind of prejudice filled his heart? These were the questions that became an independent area of research for us. The longer we worked, the clearer it became that Abhiram Das had an extremely ordinary childhood, growing up in extreme penury and culminating, as ordinary childhoods often do, in an early adult rebellion that shook his family as much as his own life. But he could never become a true rebel. For the spirit that propelled his rebellion against injustice in his family when he was nearly twenty-five years old could not live long, though it influenced his life in a critical way in so far as it led to his complete detachment from his parents and turned him onto the path leading to asceticism. Even in asceticism he longed less for spiritual attainment and seemed more filled with worldly aspirations.[7]

Abhiram Das was born Abhinandan Mishra in 1904 in a poor Maithil Brahmin family in village Rarhi in the Darbhanga district of Bihar. He was the eldest of seven children. Due to landlessness and unemployment, his family could barely afford two square meals a day. His father Jaidev Mishra considered the idea of physical toil to earn wages beneath him and used to perform religious rituals for the villagers in the small village temple. On occasions such as marriages and funerals, he would visit the villagers too, and the offerings he got formed the only source of income for the family. To run such a large family on this meagre and irregular income was almost impossible for Abhinandan's mother Thakkain Devi who always looked undernourished and ailing.

Yet, despite the penury and grim living conditions, Jaidev Mishra used to take great pride in being the father of six sons and a daughter. They all loved the youngest one, a baby girl named Batahi (meaning scatterbrain), who was almost twenty years younger to Abhinandan. Though his father wanted him to study and got him admitted in a school, Ahinandan was an unwilling student and soon dropped out, having barely finished Class I. From the age of seven, Abhinandan began accompanying his father to the village temple, collecting flowers and washing utensils for religious rituals. His life remained uneventful, and year after year was lost by the family in desperate efforts to feed itself. That was the condition of most of the households in the village in those days. Abhinandan, like most other young men in the village, hated the poverty and deprivation.

However, there was a complete absence of jobs except work in the fields. For Abhinandan, the son of a Brahmin, this option was not feasible in his own village. But he found a way out of the conundrum. One morning, when it was still dark and his entire family asleep, he left the village, convinced he would return after earning some money to improve the condition of the family and marry off his sister who at that time was merely a year old. Soon Abhinandan, who was in his early adulthood, reached a distant village where nobody knew his caste identity. Taking up any work he was offered, he started saving for his family and for his sister's wedding. He toiled in fields, looked after farmers' cattle, worked with shopkeepers and fetched grain and other commodities from various places. All this while, he dreamt of going back home with his earnings and offering a good life to his siblings and parents, and so, for five years, he kept slogging in distant villages and towns and took up all kinds of occupations.

It was around this time that Abhinandan's life took yet another turn. One day, the news reached him that his father, quite suddenly and apparently without much warning, had decided to sell Batahi Dai, his sister, in marriage to an old man. Batahi at that time was merely six years old. The news left Abhinandan infuriated. Among Maithil Brahmins, it was an age-old custom for poor families to give their daughters, often minors, in marriage to bridegrooms who offered a price for the bride. Such marriages were usually arranged between highly incompatible couples, the grooms in such marriages being either handicapped or very old. Only one thing was common to all of them – they were rich.

Abhinandan had never wanted his sister to fall victim to this custom. Five years back, before leaving home, he had asked his father not to sell off his sister and had promised that 'instead of taking money from the bridegroom, we will pay for the marriage of Batahi Dai'.

Abhinandan immediately set out for his village to stop what was about to happen. But when he reached home, he found that Jaidev Mishra, who had already taken Rs 200 from the groom, was determined to go ahead with his decision. There were angry exchanges between father and son. Batahi Dai was not even aware of what was happening. Abhinandan could not bear to look at her. The marriage was to take place the next day. The entire affair seemed extremely bizarre, and cruel.

This was the decisive moment in his life. That night, Abhinandan left his home in protest. His father remained unperturbed and went ahead with his decision and the wedding took place as per schedule. Three days later, Batahi Dai left the village with her 'husband'. Merely months after the marriage, the husband – a resident of village Khutauna which was about 40 kilometres north-east of Rarhi – passed away. The young girl was now a child widow and that too in a traditional Maithil Brahmin family. Batahi Dai was sent back to her paternal village within six months. Life was hard and painful for the young girl, and everyone shed tears, though no one could ever speak against the torture she suffered in and after marriage. Batahi Dai was to live a very long life; she died only in 2005.

For a few years after leaving home, Abhinandan remained utterly confused about where he should go and what he should do. Penniless and with nothing to call his own, he went to Patna, the state capital of Bihar. His education had made him barely literate, and he had no skills either. The only possession he had was crude physical strength – Abhinandan was over six feet tall and had a sculpted physique. He started taking up all kinds of manual jobs in the city.

But he got tired very soon and, after a protracted period of acute personal stress and financial insecurity, decided to become a priest in a small temple somewhere in Patna. No one knows for sure which temple it was and what really led him to become a priest – a genuine spiritual quest and desire to reach God or his belief that being a Brahmin and the son of a priest, it wouldn't be too difficult to perform religious rituals. It seems Abhinandan had no spiritual inclination at that time, nor was he even remotely concerned with religious and philosophical discourses. He was interested only in having an easy life with a bit of dignity that could promise him an escape from the hardships he had suffered while doing manual labour. In his childhood, he had assisted his father in performing religious rituals in the village temple and in the process had learnt a few Sanskrit verses as well. That skill might have given him the confidence to switch over to his paternal occupation.

However, the priesthood he opted for did not go smoothly either. There were times when no offerings came. And when they did, Abhinandan could never partake of them, for the main priest in the temple had an eagle eye set on each and every offering that came in. For all his labour, Abhinandan merely got food and shelter at the temple.

For some time, his life continued like that. Then one day in the same year that a massive earthquake struck Bihar – as he later told his disciple Satyendra Das – Abhinandan reached Ayodhya. The colossal earthquake he referred to had occurred on 15 January 1934 and had devastated a wide geographical area stretching from Allahabad to Darjeeling and from Kathmandu to Patna. The death toll was estimated at 20,000.[8] Districts in north Bihar, including Darbhanga (in which Abhinandan's paternal village was located) suffered the most number of casualties. Patna, too, was badly hit. At the time, Abhinandan was nearly thirty years old.

No one, however, knows what brought him to Ayodhya and prompted him to become a sadhu. He never talked to any of his disciples or his brothers and cousins about the motivations that acted upon him at this point of time. Although it is difficult to arrive at a definite explanation for Abhinandan's decision to opt for a life of renunciation, his younger brother Upendranath Mishra and cousins Awadh Kishore Jha and Indushekhar Jha believe that the reason might have been more mundane than spiritual. Indeed, from the beginning, Abhinandan seems to have pursued a single-track career – that of an ordinary man never interested in scholarly or philosophical pursuits but always looking for means of sustenance. The earthquake, by devastating almost the whole of Bihar, might have made life even more difficult for ordinary people. The quest for an alternative means of sustenance had perhaps been instrumental in bringing Abhinandan to Ayodhya where he might have found in a life of asceticism a convenient and socially recognized 'escape' from acute personal stress and dissatisfaction with worldly life. For, in the given circumstances, whatever rigours and deprivations an ascetic life might have represented, it correspondingly offered certain compensations too. It definitely provided, for instance, a form of financial security that was sometimes greater than the kind possible in many worldly occupations.

Asceticism continues to exist as an alternative lifestyle and strategy for personal survival for many from poverty-stricken parts of the Gangetic plain who are either incapable of dealing with life in any other way or who do not wish to live within the narrow confines of the domestic setting of family, kin, caste and village. The sense of support and security that the incorporation into an ascetic sect offers might well have been much greater in 1934 – when a good part of the Gangetic plain lay flattened by the earthquake – than it is today. Additionally for Abhinandan, the detachment from his family following his failure to prevent his little sister from being sold off by his father must have acted upon his decision to enter into an ascetic sect.

Whatever be the case, Abhinandan did indeed tell his disciples about his first encounters in Ayodhya as well as the process of his initiation into an ascetic life. For the first few days after coming to Ayodhya, Abhinandan walked aimlessly around town, hopping from one temple to the other, eating in bhandaras and sleeping on the ghats of the Sarayu. One morning, as he sat outside the temple of Lord Hanuman in Hanumangarhi after taking a bath in the Sarayu, he saw a very impressive-looking sadhu staring at him intently. The ascetic was stoutly built, had long matted hair and a grey beard, wore a pure white cotton garment, and carried a long iron-tipped lathi.

He beckoned to Abhinandan to come over to him and asked if he was a resident of Ayodhya and what he was doing there. Abhinandan told him that he was new to the town and had been staying on the ghats of the Sarayu for the past few days. The sadhu then asked him if he had a guru and if he was doing any sadhana. The reply was in the negative. The sadhu said that Abhinandan seemed to have the desire and lakshanas for a devotional life and advised him to accept his initiation from a guru and receive a mantra in order to be protected and guided on the spiritual path. He told him that his name was Saryu Das and that he had an asan in Hanumangarhi. He then invited Abhinandan to come and live with him in his asan and offered to take care of his needs such as food and clothing.

Unsure what to make of this offer, Abhinandan stood there for a while. But as the sadhu turned to leave, Abhinandan expressed his willingness to become his disciple and accompanied him to his asan. A few weeks later, Abhinandan had his head shaved except for a top knot, called shikha, and went through an elaborate initiation ceremony. A new name, symbolic of his ascetic status and sect affiliation, was bestowed upon him. Abhinandan Mishra thus became Abhiram Das, the name he used for the rest of his life.

Abhinandan, however, did not receive the mantra from Saryu Das. The reason was rather odd. Theoretically, sadhus do not have a caste. But in Ayodhya, the caste system is as much in vogue among sadhus as among grihasthas. Saryu Das belonged to a backward caste called Yadav, while Abhinandan Mishra was a Brahmin. Saryu Das, therefore, got him initiated by Jamuna Das, a Brahmin sadhu of his own sect.

In this way, Abhiram Das had two preceptors – Saryu Das, with whom he lived and whose asan in Hanumangarhi he inherited after his death, and Jamuna Das, who initiated him and gave him the sacred mantra and a new name and who in that capacity became a father figure for him.

For almost a decade after becoming a sadhu, Abhiram Das remained completely cut off from all his acquaintances, but sometime in 1944, one of his younger brothers, Shrikrishna Mishra, succeeded in finding him again. Abhiram Das was forty at that time. Shrikrishna Mishra informed Abhiram that their mother Thakkain Devi had died a few weeks ago and persuaded him to visit the village with him. He also informed him that their father Jaidev Mishra had died two years earlier, in 1942.

When Abhiram Das reached his village, his first visit in fifteen years, his brothers and his widowed sister, who now lived in Rarhi, pleaded with him to give up the life of an ascetic and come back. But Abhiram Das was thoroughly committed to remaining a sadhu by this time and had no desire to ever be a householder. Finally, after much debate, he succeeded in convincing them of his intentions.

Abhiram Das did not remain long in his village, but he never snapped the contact with his siblings and villagers thereafter. At his suggestion, three of his younger brothers – Chhabilal Mishra, Shrikrishna Mishra and Upendranath Mishra – went to Ayodhya and started studying there. Later, some of his cousins, including Yugal Kishore Jha, Awadh Kishore Jha and Indushekhar Jha, also joined Abhiram Das's brothers, who were to take care of all of them.

After this, Abhiram Das led a somewhat unorthodox life. Unlike other sadhus, he maintained a fairly constant relationship with his siblings and cousins, thus juggling two contrasting lifestyles, that of a householder and a renunciate. He also started taking a keen interest in the management of the real estate owned, or rather controlled, by Hanumangarhi in Ayodhya as well as in accumulation of property for himself. Very soon he became an enthusiastic member of the All India Hindu Mahasabha as well, always spewing venom at Muslims, holding them responsible for all the ills afflicting Ayodhya and spending most of his time with the Hindu communalists of the town.

Yet it is not certain whether, while planting the idol of Lord Rama in the Babri Masjid, Abhiram Das was aware of the larger conspiracy of the Hindu Mahasabha leaders or if he was merely a willing pawn in the hands of those who expected the night of 22 December 1949 to kick off a massive process of de-Congressization and create the foundation for a Hindu Rashtra. It would have become clear had the government swooped on the conspirators as it did after the assassination of Mahatma Gandhi just two years earlier.

On the face of it, Abhiram Das, a foul-mouthed, ill-tempered and almost completely illiterate sadhu, did not appear to be a conspirator who might have been part of the league of leaders secretly planning to change the destiny of India. The story of the conspiracy, as it emerged in the course of our research, revolved largely around Mahant Digvijai Nath – the powerful president of the Hindu Mahasabha unit in the United Provinces – who became the party's national general secretary just two days after the Babri Masjid incident. That the mahant, one of the prime accused in the Gandhi murder case, could achieve this just months after being acquitted on the grounds of insufficient evidence is in itself indicative of the state government's attitude towards the activities of a communal organization like the Hindu Mahasabha and its leaders.

It seems likely that Abhiram Das, who was mentioned as the main accused in the FIR registered on 23 December 1949, as well as the charge sheet filed forty days later (on 1 February 1950), played the role of a spear-carrier waiting in the wings until summoned by his masters – the mahant and some other leaders of the Hindu Mahasabha – to carry out their orders. These masters, the real conspirators, never figured in the list of accused, partly because the top district officials were themselves heavily involved in the conspiracy, and partly because the state government saw in this development in Ayodhya a strengthening of its own position vis-à-vis the secularists in the Congress.

IV

That also explains why a complete darkness was allowed to fall on the night of 22 December 1949 and why the incumbent government of the United Provinces remained unwilling to probe the matter. The lack of an authorized inquiry into the incident does not, however, mean a complete absence of primary sources and local remembrance. In fact, with a little effort and persistence, we succeeded in locating some of the critical eyewitnesses too. What surprised us was that they had never been approached by anyone trying to breach the wall of silence erected by history during the intervening six decades. The accounts of many more eyewitnesses could have been obtained and preserved had they been reached before they passed away.

This book details one dramatic occurrence – the appearance of the idol in Babri Masjid in the intervening night between 22 and 23 December 1949. Our major concern, in the course of our research and fieldwork, has been to throw the maximum light possible on that fateful night. As the conspiracy was part of the plot to gain control of the mosque, the book examines this as well.

In the beginning, we were searching for the buried narrative of Abhiram Das, the man whose action on that fateful night has had such a long-lasting impact on the nation, its politics and society, and yet about whom almost nothing was known except that he was a sadhu of Ayodhya and a resident of Hanumangarhi. Till then we had no inkling about the larger conspiracy that had made that night possible.

In October 2010, while talking to Acharya Satyendra Das, the chief priest of the Ramajanmabhoomi Temple, we got to know that his guru Abhiram Das was born in a village called Rarhi in Bihar. He was, however, not certain as to whether this village is now part of the district of Darbhanga or of Samastipur. Unsure of whether Rarhi still existed, it took us a few weeks to locate three villages by this name in the two districts – two in Darbhanga and one in

Samastipur. It now seemed possible to zero in on the village we had been searching for. A little more effort led us to our destination; the village where Abhiram Das was born in 1904 is part of Jale block in the district of Darbhanga. The precise details regarding Abhiram Das and his silent exit from Rarhi have been erased by time, but the impression of his rebellion was still strong and clear in the memory of many of the senior residents of the village.

Abhiram Das's youngest brother, Upendranath Mishra, as well as his cousin, Awadh Kishore Jha, were still living in the village. They were in Ayodhya in 1949, staying at the Ramghat temple on the banks of the Sarayu. Two days of interactions with them in November 2010 made it clear that the story of the night of 22 December 1949 is much more nuanced than being just the buried narrative of a sadhu. It was in Rarhi that we saw the first, though extremely faint, glimpse of the conspiracy – a glimpse that at once transformed the entire orientation as well as the scope of our research. We had never expected that the incident of that night was anything more than a locally engineered dark spot in the history of modern India. But the direct involvement of those who had been some of the prime accused in the Gandhi murder at once changed our understanding of the event. It was as if the dark spot had merged with the light and had become luminous.

The conspiracy that was slowly emerging was too shocking to be believed, and it soon led us to Mumbai to interview Indushekhar Jha, another cousin who followed Abhiram Das inside the Babri Masjid that night; to Balrampur in UP for a chat with Rajendra Singh, son of Gopal Singh Visharad, a Hindu Mahasabha leader in Faizabad; and to many more destinations with a clear objective to dig out the larger story. Simultaneously, we also started searching for archival material in Faizabad, Allahabad, Lucknow and Delhi to uncover the various strands, characters, motivations and collaborators in this conspiracy.

In the end, historical fieldwork and the narratives emerging out of it proved to be as important as the collection of archival material in Delhi and other places. Now the entire story, obscured for over half a century, was before us. It was the story of various motivations reaching fruition with a larger communal agenda. It was the story of not just a single overarching conspiracy hatched by Hindu communalists, but also of a series of tiny plots that got intricately woven into it – all of which came together to set up one of the most fateful nights in modern Indian history.

Prologue

9 A.M., 23 DECEMBER 1949. Hours after the idol of Lord Rama appeared in the Babri Masjid, Pandit Ramdeo Dubey, officer-in-charge, Ayodhya Police Station, Faizabad, UP,[1] lodged an FIR against Abhiram Das, Ram Sakal Das, Sudarshan Das and fifty to sixty other persons, whose names were not known, under Sections 147 (rioting), 448 (trespassing) and 295 (defiling a place of worship) of the Indian Penal Code (IPC). The FIR stated:

> That at about 7 in the morning when I [Ramdeo Dubey] reached the Janmabhoomi, I came to know from Mata Prasad [Constable No. 7, Ayodhya Police Station] that a group of 50 to 60 persons have entered the Babri Masjid by breaking open the locks of the compound and also by scaling the walls and staircases and placed an idol of Shri Bhagwan in it and scribbled sketches of Sita, Ramji, etc. in saffron and yellow colours on the inner and outer walls of it. That Hans Raj [Constable No. 70, who was on duty at the time when 50–60 persons entered] stopped them [from doing so] but they did not care. The PAC [Provincial Armed Constabulary] guards present there were called for help. But by then the people had already entered the mosque. Senior district officials visited the site and got into action. Later on, a mob of five to six thousand people gathered and tried to enter into the mosque raising religious slogans and singing kirtans.

But due to proper arrangement, nothing happened. Committers of crime [Abhi]Ram Das, [Ram] Sakal Das, Sudarshan Das with 50 to 60 persons, names not known, have desecrated [naapaak kiya hai] the mosque by trespassing the mosque through rioting and placing idol in it. Officers on duty and many other people have seen it. So the case has been checked. It is found correct.

CHAPTER 1

'Maharaj ... Follow Me'

11 P.M., 22 DECEMBER 1949. Moments before Abhiram Das[1] stood at the threshold of the temple at Ramghat, Ayodhya slept in peace. Although it was barely eleven in the night, the township, located at the edge of Faizabad, had passed into deep slumber. The night was cold, and a layer of still air covered Ayodhya like a blanket. Feeble strains of Ramakatha wafted in from the Ramachabutara. Perhaps the devotees keeping the story of Lord Rama alive were getting tired and sleepy. The sweet murmur of the Sarayu added to the deceptive calm.

The temple at Ramghat on the northern edge of Ayodhya was not very old. The initiative to erect it had been taken just a decade ago. But the enthusiasm did not appear to have persisted, and the construction had been halted halfway. The structure remained small in size and the absence of the desperately required final touches made it look crude but for the grand, projecting front facade and the rooms on both sides of the garbhagriha. In the backyard was a mango grove, unkempt, untended. About a kilometre away, River Sarayu, the lifeline of Ayodhya, flowed along with sandy stretches on both sides of its shoreline.

Abhiram Das stumbled as he climbed the half-built brick steps, lost in the shadows of the dimly lit lamp hanging on the wall, but recovered and entered the side room of the temple. The Ramghat temple was the prized possession of Abhiram Das, who himself lived a kilometre away in a one-room tenement that formed part of the complex of Hanumangarhi, a fortress-like structure in the heart of Ayodhya. Within the precincts of its imposing walls, there was an old, magnificent temple dedicated to Lord Hanuman. The circular bastions on each of the four corners of Hanumangarhi enhanced its structural elegance and artistic grandeur. Around the fortress and as part of the complex, there were rooms for sadhus, a Sanskrit pathshala and a huge, narrow stretch, where there was a gaushala, beside which Abhiram Das lived, close to the singhdwar of Hanumangarhi.

That, however, was only a night shelter for him. In his waking hours, Abhiram Das had innumerable engagements, and the temple at Ramghat always figured prominently among them. Not just because it was under his control, but because it housed his three younger brothers and four cousins, most of whom were enrolled with the Sanskrit pathshala in Hanumangarhi. Two of his cousins, Yugal Kishore Jha and Indushekhar Jha, as well as Abhiram's younger brother, Upendranath Mishra, were students of Maharaja Intermediate College in Ayodhya. Abhiram Das's relatives lived in the rooms adjacent to the garbhagriha and survived on offerings made by devotees to Lord Rama. They cooked for Abhiram as well. Thrice a day, they would carry his food to his room, braving the scorching sun in summer, icy winds in winter, and downpours during the rainy season. Abhiram's closeness to his extended family was unexpected in a sadhu. The ascetic in him often cautioned against such human weaknesses, but it had always been beyond him to transcend them.

Yet, visiting Ramghat temple that night was not part of his original plan as he set out to install the idol of Lord Rama inside the sixteenth-century mosque. Nor were his brothers and cousins used to seeing him at this odd hour in his second home. For, like any other sadhu, he was in the habit of going to bed and getting up early.

Indeed, it was awkward for Abhiram Das too. He had to change his original plan owing to the sudden disappearance of his friend Ramchandra Das Paramhans, who was supposed to accompany him in his surreptitious mission.

Abhiram and Paramhans were old friends. They shared a common ideology – both were attached to the All India Hindu Mahasabha (while Abhiram was an enthusiastic member of the party, Paramhans was its city president) and occupied a position somewhere right of the centre in this political outfit that had come under immense pressure following the assassination of Mahatma Gandhi by Nathuram Godse.

'There was also a basic difference between the two,' recounts Awadh Kishore Jha, one of the cousins of Das and part of the study circle at Ramghat Temple in 1949. 'While Ramchandra Das Paramhans was an educated person proficient in Sanskrit, the Vedas and Indian scriptures, Abhiram Das was almost illiterate and could barely write his name.' Awadh Kishore, now over eighty years old, left Ayodhya after completing his studies in early 1950s and returned to his village Rarhi in the Darbhanga district of Bihar.[2]

According to the plan, Paramhans was to arrive at the Hanumangarhi residence of Abhiram Das by 9 p.m., after his meal. They were to go together to the Babri Masjid, where another sadhu, Vrindavan Das, was to join them with an idol of Lord Rama. The trio was then supposed to go inside the sixteenth-century mosque, plant the idol below its central dome and keep the deserted place of worship under their control till the next morning when a larger band of Hindu communalists would pour in for support. They had been strictly instructed that their entry into the mosque had to be completed at any cost before midnight – the time when there would be a change of guard at the gate of the mosque.

Every detail had been planned meticulously, and everything seemed to be moving accordingly, till Ramchandra Das Paramhans vanished from the scene. Forty-two years later, when none of those involved in planting the idol was alive to contradict him, Paramhans sought to appropriate history. 'I am the very man who put the idol inside the masjid,' Paramhans declared in a news report that appeared in the *New York Times* on 22 December 1991.[3]

However, on that fateful night of 1949 and for a few days thereafter, Paramhans went missing from the scene in Ayodhya. Indushekhar Jha who, together with Yugal Kishore Jha, followed Abhiram Das into the mosque, had this to say about Paramhans: 'I saw Paramhans in the evening [of 22 December 1949]. Thereafter, he was not seen in Ayodhya for [the] next three days. Yet it was he who took maximum advantage from that incident.'[4]

Nor did Awadh Kishore remember seeing Ramchandra Das Paramhans in the mosque early next morning when curiosity led him to the spot as early as 5 a.m. Awadh Kishore recalled what his elder brother, Yugal Kishore Jha, had told him many years later:

> Baba Abhiram Das and Paramhans used to be together most of the time during the months before the installation of the idol. I was therefore surprised not to see him in the Babri Masjid early next morning [on 23 December 1949] when I reached the spot. Later, I asked Yugal Babu about this puzzle. He told me that Baba Abhiram Das was shocked when Paramhans disappeared on the night of 22 December because the original plan was that they would go inside the mosque together and carry out their secret mission.[5]

There is no precise evidence to suggest exactly where Ramchandra Das Paramhans went that evening. Many senior residents of Ayodhya as well as Awadh Kishore believe that on the evening of 22 December, without informing Abhiram Das, he left town to attend the three-day conference of the All India Hindu Mahasabha that was scheduled to begin on 24 December in Calcutta. As for the reason for his sudden decision to leave Ayodhya and participate in the conference instead of accompanying Abhiram Das, nothing can be said for sure except that he may have been apprehensive of the consequences of the act. On his part, Ramchandra Das Paramhans, after having taken credit in 1991 for installing the idol inside the Babri Masjid, preferred to remain silent on the issue till his death in 2003.

Back in those uncertain moments of 1949, Abhiram Das waited at his Hanumangarhi residence for Ramchandra Das Paramhans till around 10 p.m., after which he left in search of his friend. Paramhans lived in a temple in the Ramghat locality of Ayodhya. It was quite close to the one inhabited by Abhiram Das's brothers and cousins. But Paramhans was not to be found there. This made Abhiram rather less confident of accomplishing the task he had set out for. The strength he had was that of faith, without any rationale to go with it. But as the moment approached, the magnitude of the job, as well as its possible repercussions unfolded with a clarity that was missing till then.

Wanting to prepare for any eventuality, he decided to give appropriate instructions to his brothers and cousins at the temple in Ramghat before proceeding on his journey towards the Babri Masjid.[6]

This is what had taken Abhiram Das to the temple at Ramghat.

II

Abhiram Das was a naga vairagi, a militant ascetic of the Ramanandi sect, for the last fifteen years. He was fairly well known, both in Ayodhya and its religio-cultural epicentre, Hanumangarhi, the baithak or the main seat of power of the Nirvani Akhara. The term 'akhara' refers at the same time to a camp, to a band of militant sadhus camping together and to a wrestling pit attached to such establishments.

During the period since 1934, when Abhiram Das came to Ayodhya and got initiated as a militant ascetic of the Ramanandi sect attached to the Nirvani Akhara, his prominence in Hanumangarhi had grown quite rapidly. He had inherited the dwelling place at Hanumangarhi from Saryu Das, the naga vairagi who had persuaded him to join his flock and had given him food, clothing and shelter. In his ascetic lineage, however, Abhiram Das was seen as the disciple of another naga vairagi of the same akhara – Jamuna Das, who had given him initiation as well as the mantra, the sacred formula.

Upon becoming a disciple of Jamuna Das, he travelled to almost all the places of pilgrimage. Yet, never did he show any yearning for acquiring knowledge through studies of religious texts, nor did anyone ever see him engaging with others on issues concerning spirituality and metaphysics.

It was the akhara, the wrestling pit, where he excelled. Such was his performance that in a short while, the residents of Hanumangarhi, and gradually all the vairagi sections of Ayodhya, knew that this man had the blessings of Lord Hanuman, the god of martial arts. His stock among the sanyasis and vairagis of Ayodhya started rising.

In naga parlance, sanyasi and vairagi designate different sectarian affiliations. Shaiva nagas – or those who worship Lord Shiva as the supreme deity and Shankaracharya (the exponent of non-dualism who was born in 788 AD and lived till 820 AD) as their Adi Guru (the original teacher), and who belong to one of the ten orders collectively known as Dashnami Sampradaya – are called sanyasis or renunciants. The Vaishnava nagas – or those who worship Lord Vishnu or one of his manifestations as the supreme deity and regard Ramananda (a Vaishnava teacher born several centuries after Shankaracharya) as their Adi Guru – are referred to as vairagis, meaning 'detached' or 'dispassionate'. (For details see Appendix I.)

Nirvani Akhara is one of the three major militant ascetic camps of the Ramanandi sect, the other two being the Nirmohi and the Digambari akharas, each with its principal centre in Ayodhya. The establishment of Ramanandi akharas in Ayodhya, however, did not take place smoothly. They first had to uproot the Dashnamis who had an established presence in Ayodhya. The

Ramanandis, after organizing themselves in a military fashion, started expanding their territory in the early eighteenth century. Till then they were apparently operating primarily in western India, especially in Rajasthan and Punjab. In the course of that century, they spread throughout northern India and established monasteries in various places of Vaishnava sectarian significance in the region.

The first such sect to come to Ayodhya – a place that had always been central in the theology of the Ramanandis – was the Nirmohi Akhara. This is said to have happened in the early eighteenth century. At about the same time, the Nirvani Akhara – led by its mahant, Baba Abhay Ram Das – is also said to have entered this holy town. Gradually, in the course of the eighteenth century, other Ramanandi akharas too established themselves at what they considered the birthplace of their supreme deity Rama.

The Dashnamis, who seem to have been well entrenched in Ayodhya at that time, were not delighted by the arrival of their Vaishnava counterparts and resisted fiercely, but ultimately, the Ramanandi nagas pushed them out of Ayodhya. The Hanuman Tilla or Hanuman Hill, the site that eventually developed into Hanumangarhi, for example, was originally in the hands of the Dashnamis. Juna Akhara, one of the most prominent Dashnami akharas, had been occupying Hanuman Tilla, but was attacked and defeated by the Ramanandi nagas of Nirvani Akhara under their leader Baba Abhay Ram Das in the eighteenth century.[7]

Legend has it that an idol of Lord Hanuman under a tree had been worshipped at Hanuman Tilla for centuries by Shaiva nagas and Muslim faqirs, the latter considering it an image of Hathile, a pir or a Muslim saint revered in this part of the country. When Baba Abhay Ram Das came with the nagas of his Nirvani Akhara, they were not allowed to worship the image and were forced to retire to their camp on the banks of the Sarayu. It is said that in the night, Lord Hanuman appeared in

Abhay Ram Das's dream and asked him to chase the Shaivites and Muslims away and build a temple in his honour because it was the site where he had stayed when Rama ruled over the region. Armed with magical powers given to him by the Lord, Abhay Ram Das was able to drive out the Shaivites the next day.[8]

Whatever be the case, under the patronage of the nawabs of Awadh, who had succeeded the Mughals as the dominant rulers in northern India in the eighteenth century, Hanuman Tilla first developed into a temple and then into a fortress – Hanumangarhi – and acquired a central position in Ayodhya. It all began after Nawab Safdarjang (1739–54) granted seven bighas of land at Hanuman Tilla to Baba Abhay Ram Das. During the time of Safdarjang's grandson, Asaf-ud-Daullah (1775–93), funds were raised to construct part of the temple-fortress on this land.[9] Soon after the nawabs of Awadh donated lands and helped in its construction, Hanumangarhi became the baithak, the main seat of power, of the Nirvani Akhara. The shri-mahant, the chief abbot, of the Nirvani Akhara became the gaddi-nashin, or head, of Hanumangarhi. Baba Abhay Ram Das was the first gaddi-nashin and the nagas of Nirvani Akhara began thronging to Hanumangarhi in large numbers. Around the middle of the nineteenth century, just when Hanumangarhi appeared to be tottering under the weight of its own nagas, the sixth gaddi-nashin, Balram Das, restructured the functioning of this centre of Nirvani Akhara on the basis of the panchayat system. Since then, the panchayat has remained the sovereign body of governance in Hanumangarhi.

Under the new system of governance, the gaddi-nashin became the titular head of Hanumangarhi and all the powers were devolved to a group of twenty-five senior and prominent nagas of the establishment, who were collectively referred to as the panchan. The panchan now became an all-powerful body that maintained order in Hanumangarhi, adjudicating any breach of conduct among the nagas, punishing them – including recommending expulsion from the sect – overseeing the property of the monastic institution, and delegating authority to subordinate officials. The gaddi-nashin who presided over the meetings of the panchan had the right to cast his vote in case of a deadlock.

Balram Das also divided the nagas of Hanumangarhi into four pattis, named Hardwari, Basantia, Ujjainia and Sagaria. He instituted a separate mahant for each patti. The entire immovable assets of Hanumangarhi, including large tracts of land in its possession, were divided among the mahants of the four pattis, though on paper the property remained in the name of the gaddi-nashin. Like the gaddi-nashin, the mahants of the pattis were also merely titular heads and the panchan patti took all decisions concerning the respective patti, including the election of the patti mahant. Later, these pattis were further subdivided into lower levels of units, thus creating a well-entrenched panchayati system in Hanumangarhi.[10]

Once the new system came into force, the post of the gaddi-nashin ceased to be transferable from its occupant vairagi to his disciple, and the panchan started deciding on the successor to the post whenever it fell vacant. To avoid any clash among the pattis, Balram Das had decreed that the post be filled by naga vairagis of different pattis by rotation. Interestingly, as per the tradition of Hanumangarhi, once a naga vairagi becomes the gaddi-nashin, he never steps out of the four walls of this fortress-like building, no matter how urgent the work; it is only after his death that a gaddi-nashin's body is taken out for submersion in the Sarayu.

The rules and regulations for the functioning of Hanumangarhi and the rights and duties of various levels of ascetics residing there were codified in 1925. By 1949, the United Provinces had emerged as one of the major areas of concentration of naga vairagis, surpassing even Rajasthan and Punjab, traditionally the prominent geographical hubs of Ramanandis. Major vairagi centres of power, or asthans, were now located in Ayodhya, Allahabad, Varanasi and Chitrakut, all in the United Provinces. There has been a lot of confusion with regard to the estimated number of vairagis in the United Provinces. According to the 1931 Census, of the total 839,285 Vaishnava vairagis, 148,285 lived in the United Provinces.[11] There was no census in 1941. The post-Independence censuses have, however, abandoned the enumeration of ascetics altogether. While till 1931, ascetics were tabulated in terms of their numbers in a particular sect, and ascetic sects were treated as if they were caste groups, in the censuses since 1951, they have simply been lumped together with beggars and vagrants.

Abhiram Das, who belonged to the Ujjainia Patti, was a member of the panchan of Hanumangarhi, which had become one of the largest religious establishments in Ayodhya. At the time, five hundred naga vairagis of the Nirvani Akhara were dependent on Hanumangarhi for food and clothing. The set-up ran comfortably on the landholdings and donations the body received from lay devotees and patrons who kept thronging to Ayodhya, considered to be among the most sacred of religious centres in India.

The pathshala in Hanumangarhi attracted Hindu students from various parts of north India. Yet the nagas of Hanumangarhi, by and large, were no more interested in religion than the average Hindu. They worshipped Lord Hanuman every day and believed that he gave them strength, but never did they enter into any intricate theological debates. They were practical-minded, worldly people, with an absence of interest in knowledge about the basic issues of existence, a quest which is ordinarily expected to haunt any ascetic. In fact, the naga occupants of Hanumangarhi were more or less a localized and sedentary section of the Nirvani Akhara with their own interests in the local economy of Ayodhya and its subsidiary temples in and around the town. Many nagas had started getting involved in activities such as moneylending and renting out temples and establishments – with almost no institutional constraints.

III

Abhiram Das, a man of the akhara, truly shared the views and outlook of the other vairagis of Hanumangarhi. He had not wrestled for many years now; but even at the age of forty-five, he had the aura of a heavyweight and was known as a wrestler par excellence. In Hanumangarhi, as in most such monastic institutions, a sadhu can either 'inherit' a prominent position from his guru or 'achieve' it through his intellect, that is, his personal charisma, sanctity and ability to attract a large following of lay devotees. But Abhiram Das had none of the qualities or prerequisites mentioned.

Both his gurus were ordinary nagas. His own intellectual abilities were constrained by his near illiteracy. Yet, Abhiram Das had found his own way of getting prominence. He made up for the modesty of his intellect with the power of his muscle. Every morning, he would do hours of exercise before starting his daily chores. This was in no way unique to him. Virtually all the nagas in Hanumangarhi, except those who were very old or ill, adhered to some regimen of daily workout which included morning exercise, and in case of the younger ones, wrestling, devotional worship and performance of a variety of ritual austerities. What made him extraordinary was his well-built body that turned him into a fearsome naga.

In fact, Abhiram Das firmly believed that intellectual knowledge could be a hindrance to someone trying to attain prominence in Hanumangarhi.[12] Of his three disciples (Dharam Das, Satyendra Das and Ramvilas Das, the last of whom later added 'Vedanti' to his name), it was Dharam Das who was closest to his heart. For it was Dharam Das who, like him, was inclined towards wrestling while his other disciples spent more time studying Sanskrit and the Vedas. Once, Dharam Das expressed his desire to study along with Satyendra Das, but Abhiram Das denied him permission saying, 'Ninety-eight per cent of Indians are illiterate; only two 2 per cent are intellectuals. Therefore, it is better to lead the majority than to wander among intellectuals like a fool.' That being his attitude towards acquiring intellectual knowledge, it was not surprising that he made Dharam Das and not Satyendra or Ramvilas his successor and transferred to him, in 1981, all the properties he had acquired through his physical prowess.

It does not, however, follow automatically that by abhorring intellectual knowledge, Abhiram Das sought to acquire a wealth of spiritual or intuitive knowledge based on his inner experiences. As was the case with most nagas residing in Hanumangarhi, the acquisition of landed property and appropriation of economic power – perhaps more than any other factor – influenced the character of Abhiram Das. Although he was an ordinary naga, his physical prowess was such that no one dared challenge him. Not that there was no resentment over his high-handed behaviour. Most nagas disliked his bullying and, occasionally, some even conspired to prevent him from getting his quota of ser-siddha, but never did they succeed in their conspiracies against this one-man army.

Of all the properties he had acquired, the temple at Ramghat where his brothers and cousins lived held special significance for him. For it was a place where he could feel at home and where he could take decisions without any inhibitions.

It was this abode of faith and solace that Abhiram Das entered on the night of 22 December 1949, a few minutes before 11 p.m., after being pushed to the edge by his co-conspirator Ramchandra Das Paramhans. As an akharamal vairagi, Abhiram Das knew that going back was simply not possible. It was worrying because only a few hours back, Paramhans, a naga vairagi belonging to the Digambari Akhara, had looked so confident. Abhiram Das was unable to figure out what might have happened to the man who had been assigned to be his fellow-traveller.

He no longer had a chance to grab the advantage that Paramhans had availed of. If he changed his mind, the plan would not just receive a setback, as had happened following the disappearance of Paramhans, it would simply fall apart. And with this would disappear a critical opportunity to turn around the affairs of Ayodhya.

For Abhiram Das, it was significant not only to gain control over the sixteenth-century mosque from the Muslims but also to establish the Nirvani Akhara's complete sway over Ayodhya. It was an established tradition that the Nirvani Akhara possessed the temple of Lord Hanuman inside Hanumangarhi, meaning, thereby, that it would have control over all the offerings and donations that the temple received from devotees and patrons. As part of this arrangement, the Nirmohi Akhara, another prominent Ramanandi akhara, had been assigned control over the Ramachabutara. The Ramachabutara until then was worshipped as Lord Rama's janmabhoomi. Accordingly, all the offerings at this site were collected by the Nirmohi Akhara.

The claim of the Nirmohi Akhara over the janmabhoomi would automatically be diluted if Abhiram Das, a member of the Nirvani Akhara, succeeded in installing an idol of Lord Rama inside the Babri Masjid – almost 50 feet away from the Ramachabutara. The 'real janmabhoomi' that would thus emerge inside the mosque would make the janmabhoomi owned for almost a century by the Nirmohi Akhara redundant. And by becoming the Janmabhoomi Uddharak, Abhiram Das would have sole control over this potentially most significant spot in Ayodhya.[13]

The capture of Ayodhya from Shaivite sanyasis – accomplished over two centuries ago by the Nirvani Akhara's legendary hero Baba Abhay Ram Das – would thus be taken a step forward if Abhiram Das succeeded in capturing the 'janmabhoomi' from the rival akhara and moving it 50 feet away, well inside the Babri Masjid.

That night therefore was not just any night for Abhiram Das. The plan to gain control of the Babri Masjid was unlike any other of his earlier ones to capture temples and lands for personal aggrandizement. The probable returns this time could be much more significant. He did not want to take any chances and wanted to put the issue of succession in order before proceeding with his plan.

As he entered the room occupied by his brothers and cousins in the temple at Ramghat that night, he was wearing the usual vairagi attire – a white cotton wrap around his waist, topped by a loose white shirt. His salt-and-pepper beard and long, unkempt grey hair with a dash of white across the front made him look distinguished.

To those who still remember him, Abhiram Das had not changed much even after he gave up wrestling: tall and stout, he walked holding himself erect, with a steel-tipped, five-foot bamboo staff in his left hand and a serious look on his face. When people made jokes, he was often unable to laugh; and his manner of talking – which was light, allusive and dry – seemed highly volatile as he had the tendency to get abusive at the slightest of provocations, though he was busy counting his prayer-beads in his mala-jhola.

With so much force did Abhiram Das enter the room that his cousin Awadh Kishore Jha felt that it was some wild animal blundering inside. He recounted later:

> I lay in my bed trying to understand [what was going on]. He tried to appear confident as ever, but he looked badly shaken. A few days later, I got to know the reason. The disappearance of Ramchandra Das (Paramhans) had shaken and scared him as never before. Abhiram Das looked completely different that night. It was not that he had changed, but that some new feature had unfolded itself in his character. I had always seen him as a 100 per cent confident man. It was around 11 p.m. [on 22 December 1949]. He ordered us all to get up.[14]

While the occupants of the room were getting out of bed, Abhiram Das kept pacing up and down, quivering – apparently with the strength of the emotions stirring within him. In one hand, he held the long bamboo staff, while the other instinctively fumbled with the beads in the mala-jhola.

As they got up, he asked his younger brother Upendranath Mishra to hold the hand of Yugal Kishore Jha, the eldest of his cousins there, and said, 'Listen to me carefully. I am going and may never return. If something happens to me, if I don't return till morning, Yugal will be my successor and in charge of this temple.'[15]

Yugal Kishore Jha pulled his hand back and stared at him incredulously. 'What on earth are you up to, maharaj?'

But Abhiram Das said nothing, nor did he look at anyone. Having put the succession issue in order, he was ready to resume his mission. He rushed out of the room and then the temple, and with rapid strides, dissolved into the darkness. His cousins Yugal Kishore Jha and Indushekhar Jha followed him, completely clueless about what was happening.

It took them hardly ten minutes to reach the spot. As they approached the open area near the Ramachabutara, another vairagi emerged from the dark corner of the outer courtyard of the Babri Masjid. It was Vrindavan Das, a Ramanandi vairagi of the Nirvani Akhara, who lived in a thatched hut near the gate of the sixteenth-century mosque. A heavy cotton bag hung from his shoulder, and there was a small idol of Rama Lalla in his hands.

Abhiram Das took the idol from Vrindavan Das and grasping it with both his hands, walked past him – as if he were not there – towards the wall that separated the inner courtyard around the Babri Masjid from the outer courtyard that contained the Ramachabutara. Vrindavan Das tried to ask him something in whispers, but Abhiram Das, appearing calmer now, once again took no notice of him.

Abhiram Das stood at the end of the pathway close to the inner courtyard, staring at the walls – his sole hurdle. Then, apparently addressing Vrindavan Das, he said, 'Maharaj ...'

Vrindavan Das said nothing, just moved closer to him, eager not to miss any word of instruction that might come his way.

'Maharaj,' said Abhiram Das again, this time coaxingly. He turned his head to look at him and said, 'Follow me.' With these words, he held the idol firmly and began climbing the wall. Soon, he was straddling it.

2

CHAPTER

The Three Kingpins

IN THE LATE AFTERNOON of 22 December 1949, a few hours before Abhiram Das and his associates sneaked into the Babri Masjid, a relatively small gathering – consisting of journalists and local members of the Hindu Mahasabha – awaited the arrival of a train at the railway station of Nagpur, a city nearly 1,000 km south of Ayodhya. It was a perfect Nagpur day, cool and pleasant, a contrast to the biting cold in Ayodhya. In the train was a veteran leader of the All India Hindu Mahasabha whose supporters waited earnestly to hear from him, since he had only recently come out of his political hibernation and taken up the task of reviving the Mahasabha that had been wrecked due to popular disaffection with the party and the government clampdown on its leaders and their activities following the assassination of Mahatma Gandhi on 30 January 1948 by Nathuram Godse, a Mahasabhaite. But none of those awaiting the leader had even the slightest idea of what was to unfold merely hours later in faraway Ayodhya.[1]

The train that had chugged off from Bombay the previous night was scheduled to make a brief halt at Nagpur before moving on to Calcutta, where the leader was to inaugurate the twenty-eighth session of the Hindu Mahasabha due to begin on 24 December 1949 – the first since Gandhi's murder. This context had raised certain vital issues, and so those present at the railway station were keen to hear the leader.

As the train approached, there was a commotion on the platform. No sooner had order been restored than a figure emerged from the compartment. Dressed in spotless white shirt and trousers and a black woollen coat, the old man at the gate stood waving to his supporters. The round-rimmed spectacles that sat below a protruding forehead, partially covered by a black cap left no one in doubt about his identity. V.D. Savarkar, despite his old age and almost a year of being in custody after the assassination of Mahatma Gandhi, showed no signs of exhaustion. There was the same twinkle in his eyes behind the thick glasses as he addressed the crowd:

> Our goal of Akhand Bharat is nearer than ever [...] Mahasabha, after two years of travails and suffering, has emerged stronger with its principles fully vindicated by the events during the period [...] The talk of a secular state is absurd in a country which is inhabited largely by Hindus, and it is their proud task to establish a Hindu Rashtra.[2]

Savarkar was deep-chested, and his voice boomed across the platform. What was particularly striking was the disturbing coincidence of the purport of those words and the act that was soon to follow. For Savarkar's emphatic speech came the same day that the Mahasabha leaders of UP chose to place the idol of Rama inside the Babri Masjid. The involvement of Savarkar, if any, in the Ayodhya strategy of his party's UP unit – as an attempt to provoke a massive mobilization of Hindus – is hard to tell from the few remaining records.[3] It is true that Abhiram Das was an active Mahasabhaite who, spearheading the party's Ayodhya strategy, led the group stealthily inside the mosque on the night of 22 December 1949 with the clear objective of converting it into a temple, but there is scant evidence implicating Savarkar in this conspiracy. Of course, any such records are very unlikely to have survived; for not only would they have shown Savarkar conspiring to capture the mosque, they might have left him and the Mahasabha highly vulnerable vis-à-vis Nehru, the secular head of independent India.

That does not, however, mean that the top leadership of the Mahasabha was completely ignorant of what the party men in UP were doing in Ayodhya just before the birth of the Indian Republic. Otherwise, the party would not have congratulated itself on its accomplishments in Ayodhya in its resolution adopted at the special session in December 1950 in Poona:

> During this year, [the] Hindu Mahasabha undertook the work of regaining the Ram Janma Bhoomi temple at Ayodhya. Sri Mahant Digvijai Nath [Hindu Mahasabha's national general secretary and president of the party's UP unit], Sri V.G. Deshpande [the party's national vice president] and Sri Tej Narain [working president of the party's UP unit] went there and the Ram Janma Bhoomi shrine is now in the possession of the Hindu Mahasabhaites [...][4]

That session, in fact, was preceded by a series of political and legal activities by Mahasabha cadres in Ayodhya and in several other parts of the country. These activities, which involved most of the powerful leaders of the party, were undertaken not just to ensure that the idol is placed inside the mosque but also that, once planted, it could not be removed in the foreseeable future and that the issue could be used to the hilt for the political mobilization of Hindus across the country.

No less striking at the Nagpur Railway Station was an iron purpose that the words of Savarkar, despite his feeble appearance, seemed to convey. There was nothing unusual in what he said on 22 December, for he had talked about 'Akhand Bharat' – restoration of a united India, by force, if necessary – and 'Hindu Rashtra' (a Hindu, as against a secular, state) earlier, too. What was atypical was the confidence with which he expressed his determination to 'establish a Hindu Rashtra' just about a month before the Constitution – already finalized by now – was to be promulgated on 26 January 1950. This confidence had been missing for almost two years – in the aftermath of the assassination of Mahatma Gandhi – when the party had been left crippled and its leaders dumped behind bars.

Mere months before the assassination, the Hindu Mahasabha had proposed 'a 12-point programme for the Hindu Nation' at a meeting – presided over by Savarkar, and largely organized by N.B. Khare, the Mahasabha leader who at that time was the chief minister of the princely state of Alwar and later became the party president two days after the installation of the idol – on 26 July 1947 in Delhi.[5] The government clampdown, however, made the Mahasabhaites too scared to refer to that programme for the next couple of years.

But once the party sought to revive itself, the only way it could have gone ahead was by making another bid to present itself as the guardian of Hindu interests. Apart from the widespread communal feeling generated in the wake of Partition, Hindus now formed an even larger proportion of the population. They accounted for 84.98 per cent of the total population of the country in 1951 – the first census after Independence – while Muslims numbered only one-tenth of the total. And yet, the Mahasabha could not have gone all out to achieve its objective. It desperately needed a plank that could be used to whip up the religious sensibilities of the Hindus. The lesson learnt from the Gandhi assassination was too crucial to be forgotten – the party could take political advantage of an action only if that manoeuvre did not end up in its obliteration. Utmost care was therefore necessary to get its conspiratorial work done surreptitiously so as to insulate the party from any direct confrontation with the government. In this way, the Mahasabha could exploit the post-Partition communal disharmony without attracting government reprisal.

What the words of Savarkar at the Nagpur Railway Station that afternoon, and the actions of his partymen a few hours later in Ayodhya displayed was a clear revival of the confidence of the Hindu Mahasabha, which allowed it to take up the project it had been forced to abandon in the wake of the assassination of Mahatma Gandhi. Together, they signalled that the champions of militant Hindu communalism were once again on the offensive.[6] This was critical, especially as it was happening just as India was getting ready to adopt a Constitution that would declare it – despite the wishes of the votaries of 'Hindu Rashtra' – a secular nation.

For the Hindu Mahasabha, a political party which till early 1948 had lakhs of adherents dedicated to a militant Hindu communalism that was opposed to the non-violence of Mahatma Gandhi, the past two years had indeed been disastrous. The assassination of Gandhi had set off an enormous wave of resentment against the party and its leaders. In Maharashtra and the Central Provinces, instances of brutal attacks by angry mobs on prominent Hindu Mahasabha leaders had become fairly common. Brahmins in these states had become specific targets of popular anger because of their over-representation in the Mahasabha and the RSS. Even ordinary sympathizers of the Mahasabha fell victim to arson and loot. So intense was the popular revulsion that curfew had to be imposed at various places in these states to bring back normalcy.[7]

The murder of Gandhi in broad daylight by Nathuram Godse – a Hindu fanatic who joined the Mahasabha out of fascination with the personality of Savarkar – left Nehru in no doubt that the votaries of the 'Hindu Rashtra' were planning nothing less than a seizure of power through hate and violence.[8] He understood the motive of Hindu communalists well in time and dealt with it using an iron hand (see Appendix II). The Mahasabha was planning to cash in on the post-Partition sentiment, and expected to surge ahead with the great energy that would be generated in the wake of the assassination of Mahatma Gandhi. However, the government clampdown, the incarceration of Mahasabha leaders across the country and massive popular revulsion had almost obliterated the party.

Days after the assassination of Gandhi, as the government banned the Rashtriya Swayamsevak Sangh, the Hindu Mahasabha, in panic, publicly announced the suspension of its political activities. The initiative came from its leader Syama Prasad

Mookerjee, then a cabinet minister in the Nehru government. On 6 February 1948, at an extraordinary meeting of the Mahasabha, Mookerjee recommended that the party, in order to escape a ban, make a choice between two divergent paths: 'to break with its political activities and limit itself to social, cultural and religious problems' or 'to abandon its communalist composition [...] and open its doors to every citizen, regardless of religion, who was ready to accept its economic and political programme'.[9] Nine days later, on 15 February 1948, the working committee of the All India Hindu Mahasabha chose the first of these options and adopted a resolution to suspend its political activities. The resolution read:

> The working committee of the All India Hindu Mahasabha has adopted a resolution deciding to suspend political activities of the All India Hindu Mahasabha and to concentrate on the real *sangathan* [organizational] work, relief and rehabilitation of the refugees and the solution of diverse social, cultural and religious problems of the Hindus for the creation of a powerful and well-organised Hindu society in the Independent India.[10]

The leaders of the Mahasabha were so scared in the aftermath of the murder of Gandhi that nowhere in the resolution did they use, even indirectly, the expression 'Hindu Rashtra', hitherto the prime motto of the organization. The resolution, instead, said that the Mahasabha, which was originally conceived as a 'social and cultural organization', had been forced to enter into the political field because of the aggressive communalism preached by the Muslim League.[11] Accordingly, the resolution added, the decision to suspend political activities 'applied only to the Hindu Sabhas in the Indian Union and the Hindu Sabhas functioning in Pakistan should be at liberty to decide their own course of action'.[12]

The resolution – which helped the Mahasabha evade a ban – however, ended up intensifying the dissent within the party. As soon as the government's pressure on the Mahasabha eased, the old guard, including former president B.S. Moonje, got restive against the 'alarmist advice' of Syama Prasad Mookerjee.[13] On 8 August 1948, the working committee of the All India Hindu Mahasabha adopted a fresh resolution, renewing its political activities.[14] It was ratified in another meeting of the working committee on 6–7 November 1948. However, as the resolution did not envisage the admission of non-Hindus to the party, Mookerjee resigned in protest on 23 November 1948.

During the entire period, Savarkar—who had been arrested soon after the assassination of Mahatma Gandhi, as he was suspected of masterminding the conspiracy—desisted from expressing his views on the developments in the Mahasabha. He was eventually exonerated in the murder trial for lack of evidence to corroborate the testimony of the approver, and the case against him was dropped on 10 February 1949. Later though, the Commission of Inquiry into Conspiracy to Murder Mahatma Gandhi, set up in 1965 under Justice Jeevan Lal Kapur, a former judge of the Supreme Court of India, submitted its report in 1970, arriving at the following conclusion: 'All these facts taken together were destructive of any theory other than the conspiracy to murder [Mahatma] by Savarkar and his group.'[15]

On his part, Savarkar, despite being absolved of the charges against him, continued to remain in political hibernation. Even after the Mahasabha formally resumed its political activities on 28 May 1949,[16] he avoided political remarks for a while. And by the time he returned to politics, the party had been reduced to a small political group, desperately looking for some means to regain its former strength.

II

Not long before Mahatma Gandhi's assassination, Mahant Digvijai Nath, one of the most powerful leaders of the Mahasabha in the United Provinces and mahant of the famous Gorakhnath Temple in Gorakhpur, a district not far from Ayodhya, was already considering a fresh attempt to take possession of the Babri Masjid. The mahant might not have been aware at that time that the idea would one day become the basis for his party's Ayodhya strategy. At least, he did not appear completely confident about the practicality of the idea when he first shared it with K.K.K. Nair, the district magistrate of Gonda at that time. The mahant broached the matter on the eve of Independence at a religious function organized by the maharaja of Balrampur (which at that time fell in Gonda district). It was this uncertainty on the part of Mahant Digvijai Nath that explains why he did not follow up on the idea for over two years, till the latter half of 1949, when a series of meetings – both secret and open – and meticulous planning finally led to the planting of the idol of Rama in the Babri Masjid.

Indeed, the idea that eventually changed the politics of India, though much later than its originators had anticipated, emerged for the first time among three friends – Maharaja Pateshwari Prasad Singh, head of the princely state of Balrampur, Mahant Digvijai Nath and K.K.K. Nair. The three were joined as much by their Hindu communal sentiments as their love for lawn tennis. The maharaja, the youngest among the three, was born on 1 January 1914 and grew up under the guardianship of a retired British officer, Colonel Hanson. Studying at Mayo Prince College, Ajmer, he was trained much in the manner of most royals of the time. By the time he finished his studies in 1935, he had become an excellent horse-rider and a highly skilled lawn tennis player.[17]

Tennis, in fact, ensured that Nair, an ICS officer who had arrived in Gonda in August 1946, became a very good friend of the maharaja. Though Nair was seven years older (he was born on 11 September 1907 in Alleppey, Kerala) than the maharaja, the relationship they developed on the tennis court survived even after he was transferred out of Gonda in July 1947.

Mahant Digvijai Nath was a tall, stocky, broad-shouldered, immensely dignified man with a quiet manner and a gift for diplomacy. He was considerably older than the maharaja (by twenty years) and Nair (by thirteen years). Even on the court, his bearing was so dignified that both his tennis mates treated him with a deference due not only to an elder but to a religious head as well.

It was this bond that was on full display when the maharaja organized a grand yajna at Balrampur some time in the early months of 1947. He invited, besides Mahant Digvijai Nath, many Hindu religious leaders, including Swami Karpatri, a sanyasi who belonged to the Dandis, one of the orders founded by Adi Shankaracharya. Swami Karpatri had won respect for his knowledge of Sanskrit texts and for his oratorial skills. In 1940, he had founded the Dharma Sangha, a cultural association for the defence of traditional Hinduism, and in 1941, a daily paper, *Sanmarg*. On the eve of Independence, he began to display considerable political aspirations, which led him to found, in 1948, a political party – Ram Rajya Parishad. Apart from the religious leaders, the guests of the maharaja included K.K.K. Nair.

An article published in 1991 in the Hindu Mahasabha's weekly central organ – *Hindu Sabha Varta* – refers to the confabulations among Mahant Digvijai Nath, K.K.K. Nair and Swami Karpatri in detail. It describes how they first began giving serious shape to an otherwise vague idea that, once put into motion, eventually shook the nation:

> On the last day of the yajna, Sri Digvijai Nath – as per the views expressed by Sri Vinayak Damodar Savarkar that the [Hindu] religious places which had been under occupation of foreigners must now be liberated – discussed the idea [of capturing the Babri Masjid] with Karpatriji and Nair. Promising that he would get back to him after considering the proposal seriously, Nair left for the district headquarters of Gonda. The next day, reaching the place of yajna at Balrampur, Nair went straight to Karpatriji and Mahant Digvijai Nath, who welcomed him and asked him to sit next to them. They began discussing the issue once again. When Nair enquired about the detailed plan, the mahant laid before him the strategy to get back Sri Ramjanmabhoomi in Ayodhya, apart from Kashi Vishwanath Temple in Varanasi and Sri Krishna janmabhoomi in

> Mathura. Nair then promised Digvijai Nath that he would sacrifice everything in order to accomplish the task.[18]

It is a different matter, though, that Nair was only stating a half truth. True, once transferred to Faizabad as its deputy commissioner-cum-district magistrate on 1 June 1949, he played a pivotal role in helping the Mahasabhaites capture the mosque. It is also true that as a result of this he lost his job. But he also amassed massive plots of land in Faizabad, Gonda, and other neighbouring districts during the same period, largely using the same Mahasabha connections. This more than compensated for the losses that he might have suffered due to his Ayodhya adventure. The large-scale accumulation of agricultural land that he resorted to during his nine-and-a-half months' tenure at Faizabad (detailed later in this book) – which led to the government's forcing him to take leave and later voluntary retirement – was no less scandalous than the Ayodhya misadventure.

At Balrampur, however, the idea did not infuse any urgency in Digvijai Nath or in K.K.K. Nair. Both pretended to be serious while discussing it, but the interest was short-lived despite the serious concerns expressed.

III

Whatever be the interest evoked, this was where the idea of an Ayodhya strategy was born. At the time, there was only a bemused interest since it seemed far from perfect, and it was completely forgotten by the time Gandhi was murdered. The murder, in fact, forced the Mahasabhaites to rethink the idea and try and use it to regain lost political space. They seemed to have no other way to reconnect with a substantial section of Hindus – a precondition for their survival in a democratic society.

Like Savarkar and many other Hindu Mahasabha leaders, Mahant Digvijai Nath was also arrested immediately after the murder of Gandhi. And like Savarkar and many others, he too was ultimately exonerated on the grounds of insufficient evidence. Yet the question of his complicity in the crime – as in the case of Savarkar – was never satisfactorily settled. There was more than enough evidence that he had contributed greatly to poisoning the atmosphere and goading Hindu militants to oppose Gandhi with all the means at their disposal and, if necessary, exterminate him. Robert Payne in *The Life and Death of Mahatma Gandhi* writes how such an atmosphere had already taken shape by the time Gandhi was actually killed:

> The weeks before the murder of Gandhi there was mounting evidence that his life was being threatened by a small band of determined conspirators. At first there were only those scarcely visible signs [...]: reports of speeches made against him, an increased traffic in arms, pamphlets denouncing him [...] The evidence was substantial, but it had no clear outlines.[19]

The clear outlines, however, were drawn not by Savarkar, the mastermind behind the murder, or Nathuram Godse, the man who shot the Mahatma, but by Mahant Digvijai Nath, the powerful lieutenant of the Hindu Mahasabha's supreme leader. On 27 January 1948, three days before Gandhi was murdered, Digvijai Nath exhorted Hindu militants to kill the Mahatma. This call – the first and only public revelation of the conspiracy ahead of the assassination – is believed to have injected a sense of urgency among those who had to carry out the task. Referring to the mahant's poisonous speech, the Commission of Inquiry into Conspiracy to Murder Mahatma Gandhi observed:

> V.G. Deshpande, Mahant Digvijay Nath and Professor Ram Singh at a meeting held on 27th [of January] at the Connaught Place under the auspices of the Delhi Provincial Hindu Sabha said that Mahatma Gandhi's attitude had strengthened the hands of Pakistanis. They criticized the communal policies of the Government of India and the measures taken by the Mahatma to coerce Indian Cabinet to pay [Rs] 55 crores to Pakistan. Mahant Digvijay Nath exhorted

> the gathering to turn out Mahatma Gandhi and other anti-Hindu elements.[20]

The commission took serious note of the mahant's speech and also the fact that in the meeting, shouts of 'long live Madanlal' were raised, besides other slogans, hailing Madanlal Pahwa, a youth from Punjab and an active member of the Hindu Mahasabha, who had made a failed attempt to kill Gandhi just seven days back, on 20 January 1948. Pahwa had accidentally ignited the guncotton slab 75 feet away from the spot where the Mahatma was addressing a prayer meeting. The commission observed that not only should this have been brought immediately to the notice of the government, but that the meeting should not have been allowed to be held at all.

> The commission is of the opinion that the meeting should not have been allowed to be held. It is difficult to accept the excuse that the police came to know about the proposed meeting only at 4.30 p.m., when people began gathering. Public meetings are not called at the spur of the moment and this one had been applied for a day earlier and must have been advertised earlier.[21]

Sardar Patel, himself a fine criminal lawyer, was personally convinced of Digvijai Nath's guilt. The correspondences between Syama Prasad Mookerjee, who at that time was trying his best to reorient the Mahasabha, and the Union home minister make this fact amply clear. On 4 May 1948, Mookerjee wrote to Patel:

> I am anxious to have a meeting of the All India Working Committee and the All India Committee of the Hindu Mahasabha convened sometime in May, so that our future policy and programme may be discussed and decided upon. You have always appreciated my own delicate position in the matter [...] In Delhi, several persons are now being detained, including Asutosh Lahiri, Mahant Digbijoy Nath, Professor Ram Singh and [V.G.] Deshpande. The last three are also being tried for some speeches which were made at a public

> meeting in Delhi shortly before Gandhiji's assassination. They were also previously detained under the Public Security Act [...] I hope you will be good enough to allow facilities to all members of the Working Committee and the All India Committee of the Hindu Mahasabha to attend the meetings unless they are implicated in the murder trial.[22]

Patel's reply to Mookerjee on 6 May 1948 was detailed but terse. He refused to oblige Mookerjee, who was still his cabinet colleague:

> Militant communalism, which was preached until only a few months ago by many spokesmen of the Mahasabha, including men like Mahant Digbijoy Nath, Prof. Ram Singh and [V.G.] Deshpande, could not but be regarded as a danger to public security. The same would apply to the RSS, with the additional danger inherent in an organization run in secret on military or semi-military lines. Nevertheless, we have already decided upon a policy of gradual releases and more than 50 per cent of those originally detained have already been released in accordance with that policy. It could perhaps be safely said now that a large majority of those who continue to be detained, consists of men whose release would be a danger to public security or would lead to a resuscitation of the activities which we have banned [...] As regards Mahant Digbijoy Nath, Prof. Ram Singh and Deshpande, they made very nasty speeches on 27 January for which they are being put on trial. Their release at this particular juncture [...] would be fraught with considerable risk.[23]

By all accounts, the investigation and trial into the conspiracy to kill Mahatma Gandhi was far from perfect and made no serious attempt to put the accused behind bars. As Savarkar was let off by the court, so was Mahant Digvijai Nath. And as Savarkar was implicated by the Justice Jeevan Lal Kapur Commission, so was Mahant Digvijai Nath.

By mid-1948, Mahant Digvijai Nath, already certain of being exonerated sooner rather than later, had started making future plans – for himself as well as for the Mahasabha. The statement he issued after being released from jail revealed some of what was on his mind:

> There is some confusion in the public mind about the political programme of the Hindu Sabha. I want to make it clear here. According to the need of the hour, the Hindu Sabha has simply suspended its political activities for some time only to be revived when the situation so demands. The occasion has now come and I hope the working committee of the All India Hindu Mahasabha scheduled to meet in the first week of August will reconsider its resolution and would either take part in politics or allow its members to form some new political party on the basis of Indian culture, civilization, language and tradition.[24]

The next twenty months were to be the most difficult, the most challenging and the most controversial in Mahant Digvijai Nath's life.

IV

Mahant Digvijai Nath was politically the most cunning sadhu of the twentieth century. The game he played was carefully considered. Here was a sadhu who understood politics sufficiently to deal with the Congress on equal terms, but asserted his Hindu identity strongly enough to never be seen to grovel. His arrest in the aftermath of the Gandhi murder was significant; so too was his release in the absence of clinching evidence. In any case, the Hindu Mahasabha suffered from no shortage of plotters. What it had lacked was a shrewd politician who could link religion and politics in a manner that could provide a rallying point for Hindus. And Mahant Digvijai Nath was without question one of the most brilliant politicians of this type.

Digvijai Nath was born Nanhu Singh in 1894 in Udaipur, Rajasthan. He lost both his parents when he was barely eight. His life, in a way, began with a conspiracy by his uncle. With no family to care for him, he was banished by his uncle and thrown into the lap of a mendicant of Nathpanth, Yogi Phool Nath, who brought him to the Gorakhnath Temple in Gorakhpur.

The Nathpanthis or Kanphata Yogis constitute a sect of Shaiva ascetics outside the Dashnami Sampradaya and are believed to represent the oldest school of Hindu asceticism. The present organization of the Nathpanthis is attributed to Gorakhnath, a semi-legendary figure who is believed to have lived in northern India and Nepal sometime during the end of the eleventh and the beginning of the twelfth centuries AD. In comparison to other Hindu sects, Nathpanthis emphasize on gaining extraordinary magical and psychic power called siddhi. The term Kanphata, used to designate this sect, literally means 'split ear' and refers to the practice of piercing both ears and inserting large circular earrings in them during the final stage of initiation. This sect does not seem to have had as many followers or been as widespread as the Dashnami sanyasis or Ramanandi vairagis. The reason may lie in the sect's more esoteric and heterodox orientation and the relative lack of emphasis it places on the more popular bhakti (devotional) aspects of religious expression. The Gorakhnath Temple is considered one of the main centres of the Nathpanthis.

Back home in Udaipur, Nanhu's uncle told everyone that his nephew had been lost in a fair. He even organized a false hunt for Nanhu and searched for the boy or his body in the nearby localities and in village ponds.

At the Gorakshapeeth, however, Nanhu was trained well. After finishing his school education, he took admission in St. Andrews College, Gorakhpur. In 1920, he left his education midway and started taking part in political activities. Nanhu was never more than an average student, but he was always enthusiastic about sports, especially hockey, horse-riding and tennis, which later brought him in contact with Nair.

All along at Gorakshapeeth, Nanhu remained a quiet witness to a series of conspiracies and counter-conspiracies, accompanied by unending legal suits by sadhus to grab authority at the temple, which had a large following as well as massive landholdings. In 1932, the internecine legal warfare ended in a victory for Baba Brahma Nath, who became the undisputed mahant of Gorakshapeeth. The very next year, on 15 August 1933, Baba Brahma Nath formally initiated Nanhu into Nathpanth with the new name of Digvijai Nath. In 1935, after the death of his religious preceptor, the authority of Gorakshapeeth passed on to Digvijai Nath, who was crowned mahant on 15 August of that year.

Mahant Digvijai Nath joined the Hindu Mahasabha in 1939 and rose fast in the organization partly due to his status as mahant of Gorakshapeeth and partly thanks to his political acumen. By the time of Independence, he had become an influential member of the All India Working Committee of the Hindu Mahasabha. In 1949, when the Mahasabha was struggling to get back on its feet, he was clearly one of its key figures. He was also the president of the Mahasabha in the UP. The Ayodhya strategy that he presided over enhanced his stature even further; so much so that in the twenty-eighth session of the Mahasabha held in Calcutta, soon after planting of the idol of Lord Rama in the Babri Masjid, Digvijai Nath was elected the national general secretary of the party.

Mahant Digvijai Nath was not, however, a man to flinch from breaking traditions. Much has been made of his reluctance to live up to the traditions of the Nathpanthis, his fondness for lawn tennis, his rumoured willingness to convert the Gorakhnath Temple from a religious place venerated by Hindus and Muslims alike, and one that had lower castes as its main following, to a radical centre of religio-political power controlled by Thakurs, an upper-caste martial community. Indeed, in the tradition of this temple, he was the first to actively participate in politics. It is also true that symbols and names related to the Thakur caste became predominant in the institutions initiated at the behest of the temple once Digvijai Nath, himself a Thakur, took over this religious establishment.

In fact, Digvijai Nath never pretended to be anything other than a mahant who was more interested in politics than in religion, and who loved lawn tennis as much as he hated Muslims. Though the Hindu Mahasabha, despite keeping its doors closed to non-Hindus, generally avoided spelling out in plain language the constitutional provisions it envisaged for Muslims (as that might have invited repressive measures against it), Mahant Digvijai Nath could not restrain himself on this count. What he told the *Statesman* in 1950 was simply shocking and exceptional even by the standards of the Hindu Mahasabha:

> If the Hindu Mahasabha attains power, it would deprive the Muslims of the right to vote for five to ten years, the time that it would take for them to convince the government that their interests and sentiments are pro-Indian.[25]

He was, however, also quite willing to look beyond his party when needed. In the latter half of 1949, when he started executing the Ayodhya strategy, he knew that his party alone would not be able to accomplish the task which was potent enough to galvanize the Hindu community. For this, he needed the active participation of the nagas and vairagis of Ayodhya as well as the blind support of the local administration and his party lieutenants in the area.

Three distinguishing features of his personality helped him achieve what he needed at this juncture. The first was a strong Hindu streak in his background as well as in his thought, action and speech. This helped him – despite his being the head of the Nathpanthi establishment of Gorakhpur – win the loyalty of a majority of Ramanandi nagas and vairagis in Ayodhya, including that of Abhiram Das. This streak also earned him veneration from the general secretary of his party in Faizabad, Gopal Singh Visharad, the party's Ayodhya president Ramchandra Das Paramhans, and his tennis court friend K.K.K. Nair. The second was his great oratorical skill, which he tactfully used to instil confidence among his followers and friends, and to push for an act that the Mahasabha needed so desperately in the aftermath of the assassination of Gandhi. The third, and perhaps the strongest, of his distinguishing features was his passion for cultivating a rapport with his subordinates in the party, the administrative officials in the locality and, above all, the sadhus of almost all persuasions in Ayodhya and its surroundings.

By manoeuvring the close cabal that surrounded him, Mahant Digvijai Nath started inching towards a plan that he and his cohorts thought would kick off a revival of the Mahasabha. The conversion of the Babri Masjid into a temple dedicated to Lord Rama might have been a localized phenomenon, but its impact was designed to be felt nationwide. It is another thing that the party – which hoped to achieve political gains from the events at Ayodhya – did not manage to do so in the short term.

Yet, for the Hindu Mahasabha, the choice of Ayodhya was significant not just from the point of view of the religious importance of the area per se, but also on account of the shift that it represented in the party's modus operandi. Despite the occasional demands by the party to take possession of contentious religious places in the past, they had never been a major issue, perhaps because such disputes had never provided a basis for large-scale political mobilization. In 1934, Ayodhya had witnessed a major communal riot, sparked off by the rumour of cow slaughter in a nearby village (Shahjahanpur). During the riot, a part of the Babri Masjid had also been damaged by a section of Hindus. 'However, the Mosque was repaired and reconditioned by a Muslim contractor at the expense of the British government.'[26] The incident could not provide fodder for the lasting mobilization of Hindus even in Ayodhya. There had been a number of such instances, many of them created by the Hindu Mahasabha, but none could develop into a focal point politically even in places where the government delayed taking action.

But the India of 1949 was different. In the post-Partition period, many Congress leaders sympathetic to the idea of Hindu nationalism were carrying out projects which were highly regarded by the Mahasabhaites. One such example was the reconstruction of the Somnath Temple in Gujarat which started in late 1947 and created considerable debate in the Congress, the government, and among people in general.

The temple had been partly destroyed in the raids carried out by Mahmud of Ghazni in the eleventh century. Somnath was in the princely state of Junagarh, whose nawab had announced the state's accession to Pakistan in 1947. When Sardar Patel arrived in Junagarh on 12 November 1947 to direct the occupation of the state by the Indian Army, he also displayed his Hindu credentials and announced that the temple of Somnath would be rebuilt.[27] Explaining his decision, Patel said, 'The restoration of the idols would be a point of honour and sentiment with the Hindu public.'[28] The government decided to provide funds for this purpose but on Gandhi's suggestion it was agreed that the project be financed by public subscription.[29] The reconstruction of the temple was supervised by an advisory committee under the chairmanship of K.M. Munshi, the Union minister of supply who was from Gujarat and known for his strong Hindu revivalist sentiments.[30] The ideological positioning of Munshi had even led him pretty close to the Hindu Mahasabha in 1942.[31] He had resigned from the Congress in 1941 because he felt the party was not doing enough to oppose the idea of a separate state of Pakistan. In 1946, however, he rejoined the Congress and soon became a close confidant of Sardar Vallabhbhai Patel.

As it gradually became clear, the Somnath Temple episode did not merely strengthen the Hindu traditionalists in the Congress, it also emboldened the militant Hindu communalists, creating for the Hindu Mahasabha an inspirational backdrop, especially when it started looking for ways to overcome the stigma of the assassination of Mahatma Gandhi. The issue of Ramajanmabhoomi, it was felt, might have a particular resonance among Hindus at a time when stories of communal miseries inflicted by Partition and its aftermath remained alive.

As a political party, the Mahasabha knew the possibilities that lay hidden in Ayodhya. Yet, the idea was full of risk. A forcible occupation of the Babri Masjid could have had an effect similar to the aftermath of the Gandhi assassination, but a surreptitious capture would have been a brilliant, yet simple way of occupying the structure and turning it into an emotive issue to mobilize Hindus. The symbolism of Ayodhya would then have generated a chain reaction, emboldening the Hindu fundamentalists all over the country and completely de-Congressizing the national political agenda.

There was another reason too, though not discussed openly. Popular revulsion and the government repression had made the revival of the Mahasabha in its former stronghold of Maharashtra impossible. The party sensed possibilities in the United Provinces, where it had strong leaders, and in a state full of potentially explosive issues, the social setting had clear communal overtones, so much so that even the dominant section of the Congress had grown strong Hindu traditionalist moorings. The United Provinces, therefore, could open up a fresh chapter in the history of the Hindu Mahasabha. The party knew it; so did Mahant Digvijai Nath and his lieutenants in Ayodhya – Gopal Singh Visharad, Ramchandra Das Paramhans and Abhiram Das.

The hopes that the Mahasabha had placed on the UP were buttressed further by the flurry of actions in the immediate aftermath of the planting of the idol in the Babri Masjid. It is not without reason that these acts were supervised directly by V.G. Deshpande, perhaps the most powerful person in the party after Savarkar. The newly elected president, N.B. Khare, was never treated as more than a figurehead of the Hindu Mahasabha. In fact, the two most powerful office-bearers – Deshpande and Digvijai Nath – controlled all developments related to Ayodhya.

V

One may wonder if the Mahasabhaites would still have gone ahead with their Ayodhya strategy had the ground conducive for Hindu communalists not been prepared by the Congress in the UP, particularly by its chief minister, Govind Ballabh Pant, in the course of the campaign for the Assembly by-election in Faizabad towards the middle of 1948. The methods Pant employed to crush his arch rival Acharya Narendra Dev, a prominent socialist, in Ayodhya (which was part of the Faizabad constituency) were unprecedented in the history of the Congress. They were comparable perhaps only to the pitch that Muslim League leader Muhammad Ali Jinnah had used through a more crude use of religion to win the 1946 elections for the Constituent Assembly – a move that had made partition based on religion inevitable. What Pant created was a milder version of the same pitch – a more or less open call to the Hindus of Ayodhya to side with the Congress so that the 'atheist' Acharya, who was said to have the backing of the Muslims of Ayodhya and Faizabad, could be shown his place for not displaying reverence to the religion he belonged to. What the by-election therefore left behind was open ground for Hindu communalists to run amok. The Ayodhya strategy of Hindu Mahasabha, in a way, was now merely a corollary.

That, by no means, was the only outcome of the by-election at Faizabad; they also marked the end of the grand old party as a representative of the national movement and the beginning of the Congress as an electioneering machine, fuelled no longer by the idealism of the freedom struggle but by pragmatism in politics, with the sole purpose of grabbing power and holding on to it at any cost. It was for the first time in independent India that the Congress – which had denounced the Muslim League for misusing Islam to achieve its political objective – openly exploited the religious sensibilities of Hindus to prevent Narendra Dev from getting re-elected without bringing any substantive issue of national or regional importance into the electoral debate. This shift was crucial and, despite Nehru's sincere attempts to reverse the trend, the temptation to mix religion with politics never died down and became ingrained in the party.

The by-elections had been made necessary following the decision of the Congress Socialist Party (CSP) – which had been a factional group inside the Congress right from its formation in 1934 – to part ways with its parent organization in March 1948. The parting was the result of many factors, including rampant competition among various groups for domination over the party unit in the United Provinces as well as differences over the form nation building should take and the set of individuals who should act as its chief architects. Consequently, all thirteen CSP legislators, including Acharya Narendra Dev, surrendered their seats in the UP Legislative Assembly and Council on the grounds that they felt morally obliged to seek a fresh mandate from their constituents. These elections were set for the third and fourth week of June, and the results came in July 1948.

Acharya Narendra Dev – who took the lead in this highly ethical, if constitutionally unnecessary and tactically dubious, manoeuvre was the CSP candidate from Faizabad. Although the Congress party in UP, under the leadership of Pant and his ideologue as well as the Speaker in the Assembly, Purushottamdas Tandon, decided to wage an all-out campaign against the socialists seeking a fresh mandate from the electorates, Faizabad became their main target. Underlying this decision was Pant's perceived self-interest, since the defeat of Narendra Dev would remove the only credible challenge to his authority in the UP Congress.

There was a politically intriguing prologue to the story. Following the Congress's electoral success in the 1937 elections, Narendra Dev – who had been the most prominent leader of the party unit in UP and who also had the blessings of Nehru – could have had the chief ministership of the province for the asking. He had, however, refused to accept the fruits of his political success and organizational dominance, arguing that none of the CSP members would hold ministerial positions in any governments that might be formed. This decision had arisen from their fears that occupying government offices would breed moral and ideological pollution – a fear that, in practical terms, gave an advantage to their ideological opponents in the party. The vacuum that was thus created led to the rapid emergence of rival Congressmen in UP. One was Rafi Ahmed Kidwai, whose talents lay in organizing the party and his influence within the Congress rather than parliamentary leadership. The other was Pandit Govind Ballabh Pant, who proved to be a consummately skilled parliamentary tactician at the propitious moment. Nevertheless, Pant's rise to the chief ministership of UP after the 1937 polls had been more a matter of being given power because the socialists refused it than any successfully executed political design on his part.[32]

By the time India won independence, the Congress's politics in UP, reflecting primarily the developments which had transpired through the 1930s and '40s, spanned a trinity: the Narendra Dev–led CSP constituted the Left in terms of its commitment to fairly radical programmes of social and economic reforms, the Kidwai-led faction represented the most pragmatic and secular elements in the UP Congress and the Pant-led group consisted of conservative elements of the Congress party whose political vision contained strong Hindu revivalist overtones.

In post-Independence politics, it was this third group that firmly established itself in the UP Congress. Its members achieved this goal in phases, the first target being Rafi Ahmed Kidwai, whom it subdued by successfully employing closet communalism. This it could do simply by arousing the Hindu nationalist streak that had lurked beneath the surface of the party almost from its inception. This streak had been dimly visible on various occasions. In the late nineteenth century, for example, Bal Gangadhar Tilak and other extremist leaders of the Congress had blended Hinduism with nationalism. In 1906, Tilak had secured for V.D. Savarkar, one of his young admirers, a scholarship for study in England.[33] Ironically, this was the same year in which the Muslim League was founded. This streak had become even more evident in the 1920s when Hindu sabhas had come up in many parts of the country under the auspices of the Congress. The first important session of the All India Hindu Mahasabha was held in 1923 in Varanasi, during which the president, senior Congress leader Madan Mohan Malviya, declared that every Hindu should support the Congress.[34] The following year, it met in Belgaum while the Congress session was being held. In the 1925 session, this viewpoint was reiterated by its new president, another senior Congress leader, Lala Lajpat Rai, who insisted, 'The Hindu sabhas should make no encroachment on the province of the Congress, except so far as purely communal questions are concerned.'[35] Even after the Congress and the Hindu Mahasabha formally parted ways in the early 1930s, elements sympathetic to the communalist viewpoint survived in the nationalist party and started becoming assertive in the wake of Partition. The appalling slaughter of both Hindus and Muslims, which accompanied the division of the country, poisoned relations between men who had been colleagues for decades. Muslims were treated by many in India as enemies, as representatives of Pakistan.

It was this atmosphere of bitterness that the Govind Ballabh Pant–led faction used to sideline Rafi Ahmed Kidwai. Pant and his fellow conservative Congressmen launched a campaign to question Kidwai's integrity as a loyal, secular Congress member.[36] The campaign soon bore fruit as Kidwai, by all accounts a thoroughly secular Muslim whom the Congress apotheosized in ideological terms, fell victim to the communal smear. Pant was now the sole master of the organizational wing of the party in the UP.

The threat of Acharya Narendra Dev, however, was still lurking. Despite being the premier of the province, Pant did not have complete control over the parliamentary wing of the party in the UP. The person who could easily have become the chief minister of the province in 1937 was still seen to be fairly close to Nehru, and any change in the equation at the Central level between Nehru and Patel – Patel being Pandit Pant's real source of strength – had the potential to alter the balance of power in UP.

The by-elections of 1948 were, therefore, being seen by Pandit Pant and his growing band of Congress conservatives as the next phase – indeed, in some ways the most crucial phase – of the factional infighting. Narendra Dev's defeat in the Faizabad by-election would remove the only credible challenge to Pant's control over the parliamentary domain, just as Kidwai's sidelining had eliminated the most formidable challenge to his mastery over the organizational wing of the UP Congress.

When the battle lines were drawn in Faizabad, the first move of the Pant-led faction was to replace Siddheshwari Prasad, the designated Congress candidate (this was when the inclination was to wage a nominal campaign against Narendra Dev) with Baba Raghav Das. This manoeuvre was a shrewd attempt to exploit the religious sensibilities of Hindus in the impending contest. The decision marked a critical turning point in the evolution of Congress politics. For one, religious appeal had never before been employed for electoral purposes by the party, and for another, this decision was taken keeping electoral politics in view by those who condemned resorting to any kind of communalism as morally reprehensible.[37]

Baba Raghav Das, a Gandhian based in Deoria in eastern UP, had achieved regional fame as a saintly politician for his ascetic dedication to Hinduism. Pant's decision to hurl him into the fray was aimed at arousing Hindu conservatism against the alleged atheism and materialism of Acharya Narendra Dev, particularly in Ayodhya, the home town of the socialist leader. It was thought that Baba Raghav Das would prove overwhelmingly popular in a place whose inhabitants were preoccupied with religion and where scores of vairagis could be counted on to vote in favour of the Congress candidate. To unseat Narendra Dev, Pant made several visits to Faizabad where he explicitly catered to the prejudices and political whims of the radical Hindu sections of Ayodhya. In his speeches, he did all he could to brand Narendra Dev an atheist. He repeatedly declared that Narendra Dev did not believe in Lord Rama and that he did not wear the chhot, the tuft of hair worn by devout Hindus.[38] A report on one of Pant's election speeches, which was published in *National Herald*, said:

> The premier [Pandit Pant] said that Muslims and Zamindars and other vested interests were trying to undermine the Congress [...] He said that the Socialists wanted Hindustani in Nagari and Urdu scripts to become the *lingua franca* of India. The Congress had declared its support for Hindi and had already introduced it in the administration. This was a vital issue and the people would have to decide as to which side they would choose.[39]

With Pant unequivocally aligning himself with the Hindus, the tensions between the Hindus and Muslims that had remained dormant for quite some time began to mount in Ayodhya. The local Muslims were horrified to see the premier taking sides. This was a matter of utmost concern because merely a few months back, in late 1947, a large gathering of Hindu Mahasabhaites and local vairagis had pledged to capture the Babri Masjid by force. Following this gathering, presided over by the mahant of Hanumangarhi, Sitaram Das, Hindu communalists had started imposing restrictions on Muslims going to the Babri Masjid to offer namaz. Not only did Pant deliver explicitly communal speeches, he also rejected the attempts of several deputations of local Muslims to win assurances that the UP government would not disturb the prevailing religious status quo in Ayodhya.

On his part, once Baba Raghav Das commenced campaigning in Faizabad and Ayodhya, he distributed tulsi leaves, another symbol of Hindu orthodoxy. No opportunity was lost to point out the fact that both the Baba and Pandit Pant were devout Brahmins.[40]

The communal card that Pant played horrified many top Congress leaders. But Pant openly put Muslims in the dock. Merely a few weeks back, speaking in the Constituent Assembly on 3 April 1948, Nehru had declared that 'the alliance of religion and politics in the shape of communalism is a most dangerous alliance, and it yields the most abnormal kind of illegitimate brood'.[41] The developments in UP left Nehru deeply agonized. About a year later, in September 1949, Nehru wrote to Mohanlal Saxena, the Union minister for rehabilitation:

> [...] Indeed the UP is becoming almost a foreign land for me. I do not fit in there. The UP Congress Committee, with which I have been associated for thirty-five years, now functions in a manner which amazes me. Its voice is not the voice of the Congress I have known, but something which I have opposed for the greater part of my life [...] Communalism has invaded the minds and hearts of those who were pillars of the Congress.[42]

Polling at Faizabad took place on 28 June 1948. Baba Raghav Das got 5,392 votes to Acharya Narendra Dev's 4,080. Pandit Govind Ballabh Pant's communal card had paid off, a triumph that also meant a victory for Hindu communalists, whether inside the Congress or outside it. It had set a useful precedent for the Hindu Mahasabha and had shown militant Hindu communalists that gains could be achieved by exploiting religious sensibilities for popular mobilization in Ayodhya. This left the political field open for the communalists to embark on their Ayodhya strategy, as and when they perfected it. In fact, the by-elections had made conditions so conducive for the Mahasabha that when Mahant Digvijai Nath emerged from the Delhi jail, he did not fail to take note of the highly promising situation before him:

> I am fully convinced that no government can kill Hindu feeling [...] The recent by-elections to the U.P. Legislative Assembly have clearly demonstrated how deep is the Hindu feeling engrained in the masses; so much so that to win the elections the Congress leaders had to appeal to the Hindu feeling of the voters. I, therefore, call upon all the Hindus of the province not to lose heart. It is through trial and tribulations that success is achieved [...]'[43]

Clearly, Ayodhya had now become vulnerable, and the stage had been set for the Ayodhya strategy.

3
CHAPTER

Sakhis and Vairagis

ONCE THINGS HAD PICKED up pace in Ayodhya in late 1949, Baba Raghav Das – the sadhu-politician belonging to the Congress and employed by Pandit Govind Ballabh Pant for the political annihilation of Acharya Narendra Dev – turned out to be a vital cog in the wheel of the Hindu Mahasabha.

Raghav Das was not a man to remain a pawn in political games forever. Pant might have used him as a tool to achieve his own political objectives in the province, but Raghav Das had his own ideas, which often far outreached those of Pant. On many previous occasions, he had come across, and used, similar stepping stones. Born Raghavendra Sheshappa Pachapurkar in a Brahmin family of Poona in 1896, Baba Raghav Das joined the Congress in 1920 and made his headquarters at Deoria near Gorakhpur. He had seen many ups and downs in life, none of which stopped him from pursuing his desire to climb the socio-political ladder. After wandering for years following the death of his entire family in a cholera epidemic in Maharashtra, he had finally reached Barhaj in Deoria in 1916 in search of peace and spiritual inspiration at the feet of Anant Mahaprabhu, a well-known guru of the district. The very next year, after the death of his guru, he took charge of the Barhaj Ashram. In the words of Harold A. Gould:

> In proper Hindu fashion, this transplanted Maharashtrian Brahmin replaced his guru as the spiritual leader of the area and took charge of the ashram which his guru established. But, for the saintly politician, mastery of the ashram is usually but a stepping stone to a quest for political fame.[1]

In the course of the by-election in the Faizabad constituency, Baba Raghav Das had realized the strength of Hindu communalists and vairagis in Ayodhya and had, therefore, made it clear as to which side he was aligned with. Shortly afterwards, he went as far as to support those who demanded that the Babri Masjid be handed over to Hindus. The communal overtone of Pandit Pant and Baba Raghav Das during the by-election and the latter's growing sympathies for the Ramajanmabhoomi demand soon started taking a toll on Ayodhya. Emboldened by the apparent bias of the government as well as the local representative, many now started harassing Muslims going to the mosque to offer namaz.

Once the Hindu Mahasabha resumed its political activities,[2] it knew that Baba Raghav Das was more with it than with the secularists of the Congress party. This realization was critical, for it saw in Baba – a close confidant of the premier of the province – a friend who could be pressed into service as a protective shield in case the implementation of its Ayodhya strategy backfired and attracted serious government repression. For the Mahasabha leadership, it was necessary to transmit such an impression among its local leaders in Ayodhya at this juncture in order to rid them of the fear of yet another government clampdown, and to spur them on to implement the strategy that had the potential to revive the fortunes of the party. This was essential since most of the Mahasabha leaders in Ayodhya – whether its city president Ramchandra Paramhans or its district general secretary Gopal Singh Visharad or its overenthusiastic activist and organizer Abhiram Das – had to stay behind bars for months in the wake of the assassination of Mahatma Gandhi.

With the new alliance in place, the Mahasabha did not take much time to put its house in order and set the ball rolling in Ayodhya. It simultaneously launched a campaign to create a further schism in the Congress along communal lines. On 14 August 1949, two-and-a-half months after it resumed its political activities, the United Provincial Hindu Mahasabha passed a resolution reminding the Congress of the double standards of the government regarding the Somnath Temple on the one hand and the temples in Ayodhya, Mathura and Kashi on the other. The resolution said:

> The meeting endorsed the demand of the All India Working Committee of the Hindu Mahasabha for the restoration of the temples of Shri Vishwanathji at Kashi, Shri Ram Janma Bhumi at Ayodhya and Shri Krishna Mandir at Mathura which were converted into mosques in the Mughal times and the remains of which are still there.
>
> This meeting reminds the government that the same policy in respect of these temples should be pursued as has been pursued by the central government in the restoration and erection of the temple of Shri Somnath in Saurashtra.[3]

The resolution was widely circulated, not only among Mahasabhaites but among Congress members as well. The precedence set by the Somnath Temple became a hot point of debate in the Congress circles of the United Provinces, particularly in Ayodhya.

As the atmosphere started heating up, the Hindu Mahasabha opted for the back seat and the All India Ramayan Mahasabha (AIRM) – a cultural organization formed and controlled by the local Hindu Mahasabha leaders of Ayodhya – took over its activities.[4] While Ramchandra Paramhans was the general secretary of the AIRM, Gopal Singh Visharad was its joint secretary and Abhiram Das the organizational secretary.[5]

The temple town now began witnessing rapid developments. Realizing that the moment was ripe for taking the dramatic and historic step of carrying out its strategy, the Ramayan Mahasabha stepped up its mobilization of the naga vairagis residing in Hanumangarhi and announced a massive nine-day recitation of the

Ramcharitmanas, a popular version of the Ramayan, starting on 20 October 1949, the day of the Hanuman Janmotsava. The Hanuman Janmotsava, held on the fourteenth day of the dark fortnight of the Hindu lunar month of Kartik (corresponding with October-November), which is believed to be the birthday of Lord Hanuman, is celebrated with great pomp and show in Hanumangarhi. Such recitations, called navah paath, on the day of the Hanuman Janmotsava had been a usual practice in Hanumangarhi. So far, therefore, there was nothing unusual about it, except that in 1949 it was organized on a much larger scale than in the previous years, thanks partly to the Ramayan Mahasabha.

Only on the concluding day of the navah paath – on 28 October 1949 – did something unusual happen. In the evening of that day, the Ramayan Mahasabha organized a public meeting in Hanumangarhi which was attended by hordes of Ramanandi vairagis of various ages and hundreds of lay devotees of Lord Hanuman. Among the vairagis was a young naga belonging to the Nirmohi Akhara. Bhaskar Das, the then mahant of the Nirmohi Akhara, was in his early twenties. Six decades later, he recounted the scene of this congregation at Hanumangarhi:

> That was an unusual meeting. A large number of vairagis in their typical white attire, wearing various kinds of Ramanandi tika on their forehead, strode up and down in the courtyard [of Hanumangarhi] chatting among themselves alongside lay devotees who were often in colourful dresses. The meeting was later addressed by leaders like Baba Raghav Das, Mahant Digvijai Nath and Swami Karpatriji. It was decided in the meeting that a similar navah paath would be organized at Ramachabutara on 24 November on the occasion of Rama Vivah [the day marking the marriage of Lord Rama with Goddess Sita] in order to persuade Ram Lalla [the idol of infant Rama placed in the makeshift temple in Ramachabutara] to shift to his original place of birth inside the Babri Masjid.[6]

Not many in the audience could have realized then that the Hindu Mahasabhaites present in the meeting had rolled out a blueprint for capturing the Babri Masjid, and that the point at which the congregation at Hanumangarhi ended was when a run-up to the night of 22 December 1949 began. Significantly, it was none other than Congress leader Baba Raghav Das who moved the proposal to organize a massive navah paath in Ramachabutara on the auspicious day of Rama Vivah. In 1949, the Rama Vivah was to be celebrated on 24 November. This proposal was unanimously passed, and the meeting dispersed. A local Hindi newspaper, *Aaj*, carried the outcome of the meeting in detail:

> On the concluding day, Baba Raghav Das, M.L.A., Swami Karpatriji, head of Krishna Bodhashram, and the president of the United Province Hindu Mahasabha, Mahant Digvijai Nath, were present in the meeting. A proposal was moved by Baba Raghav Das that in order to liberate Shri Rama Janmabhoomi and for the welfare of the masses, an equally massive navah paath of Ramcharitmanas should be organized on the occasion of Shri Rama Vivah at Shri Rama Janmabhoomi [till then, the Ramachabutara, and not the Babri Masjid, was referred to as Ramajanmabhoomi]. This proposal was supported by the masses and passed unanimously. Because Hanumangarhi is the prime centre of Hindus and it is controlled by Hindus, no one dared to oppose this proposal.[7]

The Hindu Mahasabha leaders had got what they wanted despite operating from the backstage. What thrilled them further was the fact that a Congress leader and a close aide of the premier of the United Provinces had paved the way for them. Mahant Digvijai Nath had remained silent throughout, only clapping and nodding at the move that was so critical for the success of his Ayodhya strategy.

Interestingly, at no point in this period could the Baba's growing proximity with the Hindu Mahasabha come in the way of his ties with Govind Ballabh Pant who, together with Sardar Vallabhbhai Patel, was himself drifting away from the secular strand of the party led by Jawaharlal Nehru. It was only after Pant left UP to join the Union Cabinet at the insistence of Nehru in 1954 – long after the death of Patel – that Baba Raghav Das's political strength started declining. The departure of Pant meant the withdrawal of a strong network of patronage for leaders like Baba Raghav Das. Once this happened, he succumbed to the political challenge posed to him by a rival Congress member, Genda Singh, who had shot into regional prominence and had climbed up the party ladder as a leader of sugar workers in the area and who later became a minister in the state.[8]

Nehru, however, had a different opinion about Baba Raghav Das. In many of his letters written in the aftermath of the illegal seizure of the Babri Masjid, he expressed his views on the man. On 5 March 1950, Nehru wrote to K.G. Mashruwala, the editor of *Harijan*, the journal founded by Mahatma Gandhi:

> You refer to the Ayodhya mosque. This event occurred two or three months ago and I have been very gravely perturbed over it [...] It is not true that Baba Raghav Das instigated this, but it is true that after it was done, he gave his approval to it. So some other Congressmen in UP.[9]

A few months later, on 9 July 1950, Nehru wrote to Lal Bahadur Shastri, who was the home minister in the UP government at this time, with regard to the developments in Ayodhya:

> As you know, the Babri Mosque affair in Ayodhya is considered by us a major issue and one affecting deeply our whole policy and prestige [...] What distresses me most is the fact that our Congress organization takes no interest in it and some prominent Congressmen like Raghav Das and Vishambhar Dayal Tripathi carry on propaganda of the kind which can only be called communal and opposed to the Congress policy.[10]

Indeed, this was the period when two Congresses – one of Hindu conservatives, if not outright communalists, and the other of progressives and secularists – were jostling for control over the party. It sometimes seemed that the two lived not only in different mental worlds but almost in different time zones. Ayodhya was in the grip of Hindu conservatives, and Baba Raghav Das was aware of his live links – from the banks of the Sarayu to the corridors of power in Lucknow and further up to the highest seat of authority in New Delhi.

II

Whatever be the case, Rama Vivah, or the marriage of Rama and Sita, had never been a special event for the residents of Hanumangarhi. Theoretically, the akharamal vairagis practise complete celibacy and are detached from the institution of marriage and therefore, despite considering Rama Vivah an auspicious day, they do not attribute to it the same significance as Hanuman Janmotsava. It is partly because of the predominance of akharamal vairagis at Ayodhya that Rama Vivah has not been included in the four traditionally grand festivals here. These include Hanuman Janmotsava, Rama Navami (the celebration of Rama's birthday), Kartik Mela (when people come to stay for a month in Ayodhya and leave after taking a holy bath in River Sarayu on the day of Kartik Purnima when the month ends) and Jhula.

There are practical and theological reasons for Rama Vivah not being included in the list of festivals celebrated on a grand scale by vairagis and nagas. The celebration involves a real lila, or religious mystery play, complete with a wedding procession and the re-enactment of the wedding ceremony in which male devotees impersonate Rama and Sita. The drama takes a mystic shape when performed in temples. Traditionally at Ayodhya, the organizers and performers of this festival have predominantly been adherents of a rather esoteric wing of Ramanandi sadhus, called rasiks or sakhis, and whose religious life is entirely different in tone and quality from that of the vairagis and nagas. The rasiks or sakhis consider themselves female friends of Sita who are concerned about the happiness of the divine couple and who act as spectators of their marital joy. They are the most sedentary among the Ramanandi sadhus in the sense that they do not roam around in jamat, or practise the ascetic exercises of the vairagis or the military training of the nagas.

What the worship of Rama, the Ultimate Being, is to the vairagis and nagas, the worship of the divine couple, Rama and Sita, the yugal sarkar or 'the royal couple', is to the sakhis. As a vairagi or naga, a male Ramanandi sadhu will not be able to worship Rama and Sita together; he cannot, for example, bathe Sita.[11] The sakhis must, therefore, think of themselves as female friends (sakhis) of Sita. This particular set of ascetics believes that this idea originated when Rama and Sita returned from their exile to Ayodhya. At that time, Hanuman is said to have asked to be allowed to serve not just Rama, but Sita as well. It is because of this that Hanuman, who became the first sakhi of Sita, is as important to the sakhis as he is to the rest of the Ramanandi community.[12] In the sakhi version, however, Hanuman is the intermediary between Sita and the lay devotee in his, or rather her, form of Sita's principal sakhi.

Peter Van Der Veer, in his book *Gods on Earth*, notes that the male sakhis take their female identification very seriously. During worship, they wear feminine clothes and ornaments, even in public. They sometimes observe Hindu taboos associated with the menstruation period. Another matter of esoteric secrecy is the relationship between the sakhis and Rama. Although sakhis consider themselves as mugdha or unmarried girls, in many cases, their initiation as 'deeply engrossed sakhis' takes place through a symbolic wedding ceremony between them and Lord Rama. It is believed that sakhis who are initiated this way are 'taken by the hand' by Rama, who, although not openly married to 'her', can enjoy 'her' body. This leads them to further, more complicated practices, which are closely guarded secrets. Outwardly, though, the Ramanandi sakhis do not enjoy real erotic love for Rama, but help the divine couple enjoy it.

While the vairagis emphasize the period when Rama lived in the jungle as a legitimation of their ascetic lifestyle, the nagas refer to the fights between Rama and Ravana (the demon king who appears as the antagonistic character in the legend of Lord Rama) as well as to the role of the monkey army under Hanuman in order to legitimize their military exercises.[13] With such a theological backdrop, the Rama Vivah becomes an odd ceremony and concept for nagas and vairagis.

All of this serves to emphasize that the unusual nature of the decision to organize a massive navah paath of the *Ramcharitmanas* to celebrate Rama Vivah – taken at the meeting in Hanumangarhi, the central institution of the nagas and vairagis associated with the Nirvani Akhara – was rather unusual.

What made the resolution even more bizarre was the fact that Ramachabutara, the venue selected for the purpose, was controlled and managed by vairagis, a section of sadhus that would never feel at ease celebrating Rama Vivah. The nagas and vairagis attending the Hanumangarhi meeting could have opted for any of the occasions which were auspicious for them. They could have, for example, identified Rama Navami, the day on which Lord Rama is believed to have been born, or the festive days of Jhula, when the childhood of Rama is celebrated through a swing festival, to 'persuade' him to 'shift' to his 'original place of birth' inside the Babri Masjid. Above all, they could have started their exercise of 'persuasion' on the day of the next Hanuman Janmotsava, or on Kartik Purnima, when the holy month of Kartik concludes with one of the greatest bathing fairs of the year. The reason for not doing so had more to do with politics than with religion. Rama Navami, celebrated on the ninth day of the bright fortnight of the Hindu month of Chaitra (corresponding with March-April), was to be held six months later, while Jhula, celebrated in the Hindu month of Shravan (corresponding with July-August), was due only after nine months, and the next Hanuman Janmotsava would have required them to wait an entire year. Kartik Purnima, held on the last day of Kartik, which fell on 5 November in 1949, was also not viable as it offered them too short a period for preparation.

For all those in the Hanumangarhi meeting who did not want to let go the tempo that had been built up, the day of Rama

Vivah – to be held on 24 November in 1949 – was the only one that was suitable and opportune, as it was neither too distant nor too close. A distant date for putting the plan in place would have disrupted the momentum, while a date as close as Kartik Purnima would not have given the Mahasabhaites adequate time. The chosen date offered the local and provincial leaders of the Mahasabha almost a month's time to complete the preparations before they embarked on their final mission.

As for the venue, the Ramachabutara, this was going to be something unprecedented. Never in the past had the place ever celebrated Rama Vivah, and that too on a grand scale, nor had it ever witnessed a navah paath of the *Ramcharitmanas*. But then the very move to 'persuade' Rama to 'shift' to his 'original place' of birth was highly unusual, and seldom had an unusual object been achieved through usual means. Nevertheless, all through its existence, the Ramachabutara – called janmabhoomi till the planting of the idol in the mosque on the night of 22 December 1949, thus stripping this innocuous structure of its claim – had a rather weary look and could never attract too many pilgrims. Hardly surprising, given that there were rival spots in the city, which too claimed to be the real birthplace of Lord Rama.

This 17×21×6 feet platform was located about a hundred paces away from the Babri Masjid, but within its compound. It was in the south-eastern corner of the compound, surrounded by a high stone wall on the east and south. Iron railings on the west separated it from the inner courtyard of the Babri Masjid. To the north was a long and wide open space that merged with a similar rectangular stretch of the compound running from west to east on the mosque's northern side. The stone wall on the east had a gate – merely a few paces north of the chabutara – that opened to a narrow lane running straight for some distance and finally merging in the cobweb of the town.

The chabutara had, in fact, been the centre of dispute ever since it had come up, with vairagis claiming it to be the birthplace of Lord Rama, a status that instantaneously shifted to the Babri Masjid the moment the idol of Rama appeared inside the central dome of this sixteenth-century structure. That one incident changed everything – not only in the Babri Masjid compound, but in the whole of Ayodhya. And in Lucknow and Delhi and in the rest of India.

The origin of the Ramachabutara is linked inextricably to the Revolt of 1857. During the revolt, British life and property in Ayodhya and Faizabad were endangered and some landlords offered help to the British and 'a similar offer was made by the mahants of Hanumangarhi'.[14] Once the uprising was suppressed, those who had helped the British were suitably rewarded. All land in Ayodhya was nazul land, and so it was easy for the government to distribute land as reward for services rendered during the revolt.[15]

This situation threw up an opportunity for the mahants of Ayodhya. Without much delay, one of them took over a part of the Babri Masjid compound and constructed a raised platform (chabutara) there. Right from the beginning, the local Muslims repeatedly opposed this attempt. On 30 November 1858, Maulvi Muhhamad Asghar, khateeb and muezzin of the Babri Masjid, submitted a petition to the magistrate complaining that the vairagis had built a chabutara close to the mosque. Similar complaints were made by local Muslims in 1860, 1877, 1883 and 1884.[16]

On 29 January 1885, one Raghubar Das, claiming to be the mahant of the janmasthan (the chabutara), filed a suit in the court of Pandit Hari Kishan, the sub-judge of Faizabad, to gain legal title to the land and for permission to construct a temple on the chabutara. The sub-judge dismissed his suit and appeals in a judgment delivered on 24 December 1885. Six months later, on 25 May 1886, the mahant filed an appeal in the highest court in the province. On 1 November that year, the mahant's claim of proprietorship over the land within the compound of the Babri Masjid was once again dismissed by the judicial commissioner.[17]

Mainly as a result of this attitude of the courts, the mahant of the janmasthan and his successors were forced to maintain the status quo within the compound of the Babri Masjid. All those years, the Ramachabutara remained a profoundly dilapidated place with a small makeshift wooden temple and a number of small idols kept in various crevices.

The decision taken by the vairagis and the Hindu Mahasabhaites at Hanumangarhi was, therefore, something quite new. The chabutara was on the verge of achieving glory, though momentary, for the success of the Ayodhya strategy would mean shifting the focus from the chabutara to the Babri Masjid. The success of the navah paath would entail both the prospect of glory as well as the possibility of an imminent eclipse.

III

Not long before the decision had been taken, the district administration of Faizabad had got into a hectic exercise to break the status quo that had existed for almost six decades following judgments in the mid-1880s by district and provincial courts, strictly prohibiting vairagis from constructing any temple on the elevated platform. Two district officials were at the centre of this exercise. One was Deputy Commissioner-cum-District Magistrate K.K.K. Nair, who had taken charge of Faizabad on 1 June 1949. Nair had already had a discussion with Digvijai Nath – on the eve of Independence at a religious function organized by Maharaja Pateshwari Prasad Singh – on ways to convert the Babri Masjid into a temple. Nair was an outspoken Hindu communalist who, despite his official position, was openly advocating that the mosque be handed over to the Hindu community.[18]

Guru Datt Singh, the other district official involved in this exercise, was Nair's fervent supporter. He was the city magistrate of Faizabad and acted as assistant to the deputy commissioner. A Rajput by caste, he considered himself 'a man of God' and believed that the 'very existence of Hinduism' and his 'own existence' were being threatened by the Hindus who dominated the Congress simply because this party had embarked upon a programme designed to secularize Indian society.[19]

Later, the period of their stint in Faizabad proved to be their last years of government service, and they were implicated in the affair as the leaders of the Hindu militants who had planted the idol in the Babri Masjid on the night of 22 December 1949. The official investigation that ensued concluded that Nair and Singh played such a flagrant role in the incident that they must be invited to retire to private life.[20] Following this, K.K.K. Nair was forced to retire from his post together with his assistant Guru Datt Singh.[21]

It was, however, still too early for these officials to gain notoriety when, months before the planting of the idol in the Babri Masjid, they embarked on a mission to get a Rama temple erected on the chabutara through an administrative coup. Their plan was to reverse the six-decade-old status quo by obtaining permission from the state government to construct a grand temple on the chabutara and on nearby land. This, they thought, would eventually encompass the Babri Masjid.

The first thing they did for the purpose was to forward a request by some local Hindus eeking the construction of a grand temple at the chabutara to the offices of the state government located in Lucknow. In response to this request, the deputy secretary of the Government of the United Provinces, Kehar Singh, wrote a letter, dated 20 July 1949, to Nair, for 'favourable early report and his recommendation in the matter'. The letter further said:

> It should also please be stated whether the land on which the temple is proposed is a Nazul/Municipal land. The report should be forwarded to Government through the Commissioner, Lucknow Division.[22]

After receiving the letter from the state government, Nair asked his assistant, Guru Datt Singh, to visit the spot and send back a report. In his report sent to Nair on 10 October 1949, eighteen days before the decision was taken at Hanumangarhi to start a navah paath at the chabutara to reclaim the janmabhoomi, Guru Datt Singh recommended the construction of a grand temple at the site, saying:

> As per your orders, I went to the spot and inspected the site and enquired all about it in detail. Mosque and the temple both are situated side by side and both Hindus and Muslims perform their rites and religious ceremonies. Hindu public has put in this application with a view to erect a decent and *vishal* temple instead of the small one which exists at present. There is nothing on the way and permission can be given as Hindu population is very keen to have a nice temple at the place where Bhagwan Ram Chandra Ji was born. The land where temple is to be erected is of Nazul [government land].[23]

This report, thus, sought to reverse the judgment passed by the sub-judge of Faizabad, Pandit Hari Kishan Singh, on 24 December 1885 on the petition of the mahant of the chabutara who had requested permission to construct a temple on that spot:

> This place is not like [any] other place where the owner has got the right to construct any building he likes [...] If a temple is constructed on the *chabutara* at such a place then there will be the sound of bells of the temple and *sankh* when both Hindus and Muslims pass from the same way and if permission is given to Hindus for constructing a temple then one day or the other a criminal case will be started and thousands of people will be killed.[24]

In the end, however, Nair and Singh could not pull off the administrative coup they had planned. As the situation in Ayodhya deteriorated following the open advocacy of capturing the janmabhoomi by the Mahasabhaites, along with the local vairagis of Ayodhya, the state government developed cold feet, and the process set into motion by these officials could not proceed further.

That, however, did not deter Nair and Singh from pursuing

their agenda. They had already made their intentions clear. Even in its failure, the administrative coup they had planned became the talk of the town, giving a major boost to the activities of Hindu communalists. The move by these officials had increased their popularity, particularly among Hindu Mahasabhaites. In a short span of time, Gopal Singh Visharad, the head of the Faizabad unit of the Hindu Mahasabha and trusted lieutenant of Mahant Digvijai Nath, had developed a very good rapport with K.K.K. Nair and Guru Datt Singh. In the course of time, Visharad and Nair became family friends as well. They were seen together quite often, and the combination of the duo was interesting – Nair was a colossus with broad shoulders and imposing countenance, while Visharad had a short and stocky build but was agile as a fox.

Born in 1903 in Jalon, Central Provinces, Visharad was slightly older than Nair. After spending most of his childhood and youth in the nearby princely state of Samthal in the Bundelkhand region of Central Provinces, Visharad had shifted to Ayodhya in 1941. Initially, he stayed in a temple in the Swargdwari area of Ayodhya but later took a house on rent in the same locality and brought in his wife and children from Samthal. For sustenance, he opened a provision store in the nearby Shringarhaat locality.

Visharad was close to the Hindu Mahasabha right from the beginning, but he formally joined it in 1942, a year after he shifted to Ayodhya. He soon rose in the ranks of the party and by 1949, when Nair was posted in Faizabad as district magistrate, he had become the head of the party unit in the district. Rajendra Singh, Visharad's son, had this to say about Nair:

> Quite often, Nair used to visit Visharad's house in his small car, which had been gifted to him by Samthal estate. That car had a history. Before Nair, it had been used by the princess of Samthal. Once, the princess came to Ayodhya in that car and met Nair at Visharad's house. The two became friends very soon. Perhaps it was she who gifted the car to Nair, because when she left Ayodhya, Nair was seen driving that beautiful car. The development brought Nair closer to Visharad.[25]

Thereafter, the trio of K.K.K. Nair, Gopal Singh Visharad and Guru Datt Singh worked hand-in-hand to achieve their common objective, drawing inspiration and taking instruction from Mahant Digvijai Nath, who was also pretty close to the mahants and vairagis of Ayodhya, including Abhiram Das, the man who later played the key role on the ground. In a way, therefore, Digvijai Nath was acting as the unifying factor for all those who wanted the Ayodhya strategy to succeed. The clique turned out to be critical for the Hindu Mahasabha as the day of Rama Vivah approached.

IV

Just as days before the assassination of Mahatma Gandhi, Mahasabha leaders like Digvijai Nath contributed greatly to poisoning the atmosphere, so also in Ayodhya, days before the beginning of the navah paath, there was a rapid rise in militant Hindu communalism which displayed utter disdain for the faith of the minority community, as well as a willingness to use force against those whom Partition had left highly vulnerable in India. And here, too, the presence of Mahant Digvijai Nath was all-pervasive. From the district administration to the local Congress leader and member of Legislative Assembly, to the Hindu Mahasabhaites and Ayodhya's sadhus and vairagis, all were guided by the same strategist – Mahant Digvijai Nath.

The clique became hyperactive as Rama Vivah approached. Armed with Hanumangarhi's decision, the All India Ramayan Mahasabha launched a large-scale campaign to mobilize Hindus much ahead of the scheduled navah paath. Soon, the whole town of Ayodhya was in a state of panic and uproar. Muslim shopkeepers were too afraid to open their shops; namazis felt too intimidated to visit mosques freely. The Babri Masjid seemed totally out of bounds for them. It was in this fertile soil that a rumour quickly took root – that the vairagis would capture the Babri Masjid and that the navah paath would be used as an occasion to plant the idol of Rama inside it. The rumour was fuelled by the crassly tactless and utterly lukewarm approach of the district administration to the worsening situation. There was, in fact, no sign of any administration in Ayodhya, and Hindu communalists seemed to be on the prowl.

Deterioration began immediately after pilgrims had taken holy dips in the Sarayu on 5 November, on Kartik Purnima, which is observed a week after the Hanuman Janmotsava, the day when the decision to hold the navah paath to 'liberate' the janmabhoomi was taken. The navah paath was to begin three weeks later, on 24 November 1949. *Aaj* described the situation that prevailed in Ayodhya:

> After Kartik Purnima on 5 November, three Muslims went to see Babri Masjid. Some vairagis present there stopped them from entering the mosque. When they persisted, the vairagis started beating them. While two of the Muslims managed to save themselves by fleeing the scene, the third one could not do the same. The vairagis broke the limbs of this Muslim who was later admitted to Shri Ram Hospital in Ayodhya.
>
> Immediately after this incident, some vairagis and sadhus started digging the graves that were there for long in front of the Babri Masjid. Meanwhile, a rumour spread in Ayodhya that sadhus would instal an idol in the Babri Masjid. On 9 November, some local Muslims informed the district magistrate (K.K.K. Nair) about this rumour as well as the incidents of grave digging and thrashing of members of their community. The district magistrate instructed the city magistrate (Guru Datt Singh) to take appropriate action. But the city magistrate delayed the process and reached the spot only on 12 November.
>
> In the meantime, sadhus dug up hundreds of graves in the open ground in front of Babri Masjid. A small mosque, called Kanati Masjid, located to the south-east of Babri Masjid, was also razed to the ground and turned into a platform. Several havan kunds were created in places where graves were dug. Around the same time, in the south-eastern side of Babri Masjid, the mazar of Zanab Kidwa Sahab [widely believed to be the holy ancestor of Kidwai Muslims] was demolished. On a mound in the vicinity of Babri Masjid there

> used to be the famous mazar of Shah Hatta. One sadhu took it under his control and converted it into a mughara. The roof of the mughara is that of the mazar.[26]

All the signs of the storm were therefore evident much in advance, but no one in authority was willing to take note of them. And when, in the aftermath of the installation of the idol, the district magistrate, K.K.K. Nair, was asked as to why he did not take any preventive measures, his reply was simple: there was no indication of any such development. 'It was an act of which there was no forewarning,' Nair wrote to the chief secretary, Government of the United Provinces, on 26 December 1949, days after the statue was installed in the mosque. He continues:

> The last CID report which I received regarding Ayodhya affairs reached me on the 22nd [of November]. Neither in that report nor in any previous report was it ever indicated that there was a move to instal an idol in the mosque either surreptitiously or by force. Neither through official nor through non-official channels have we ever received any report of such a move with the exception that during *naumi paath* [navah paath] there was a rumour that the mosque would be entered on Poornamashi Day, but that attempt was not made.
>
> I must also mention that none of the Muslims who met me in this connection [...] ever said that there was a move for installing an idol either forcibly or clandestinely in the mosque [...][27]

Nair was obviously lying. His claim that he had no 'forewarning' and that even local Muslims never told him about the 'move for installing an idol either forcibly or clandestinely' was a desperate attempt to save his own neck. For much before the beginning of the navah paath, and more so *after* its commencement, everyone in Ayodhya sensed the combustible situation caused primarily by the activities of the All India Ramayan Mahasabha, and knew about the virtual takeover of the area around the Babri Masjid by vairagis, and the rumour that their ultimate objective was to instal the idol of Rama in the mosque. Moreover, as early as 9 November 1949, the local Muslims had sounded out Nair about it.

Ahead of the planting of the idol, however, it had already become clear that Nair, ably assisted by Guru Datt Singh, was not just sympathetic towards Hindu communalists, but was playing an active part in the conspiracy that had just begun unfolding in Ayodhya. The attitude of the two key officials towards these developments was such that it appeared to the Muslims of Ayodhya that the government either wanted all that to happen or it had succumbed to Hindu communalists. No respite was being promised by the Congress either. Baba Raghav Das was openly with the Ramayan Mahasabha, and his party had greatly changed its colour in the town, and to some extent in the state.

Not everyone in the Congress party in Faizabad was, however, delighted to see what was happening in Ayodhya. One man had the moral courage to speak up against the outrage. Akshay Brahmachari, a Gandhian who was then the secretary of the Faizabad District Congress, was opposed to the mobilization right from the beginning. He described the operation thus:

> On 13 November 1949, I was told that the Muslim graves near the Babri Masjid were being dug out *en masse*. I personally went and saw that it was actually so; and that in the centre of the graveyard, on the site of what used to be called Kanati Masjid by Muslims, a platform was being built. The Muslims were frightened. They told me that to save the situation they had petitioned the City Magistrate under Section 145 IPC to intervene in the matter, as breach of peace was apprehended. But no action was taken on their petition. I met the District Magistrate personally and talked to him in confidence.
>
> On the night of 15 November, three persons entered my house and assaulted me, and to my utter surprise they repeated to me everything that I had spoken to the District Magistrate ...[28]

Indeed, the navah paath began on a scale unprecedented in Ayodhya. The Muslim graveyard, called Ganj-e-Shaheedan Qabrastan located in the appurtenant land of the Babri Masjid, proved an easy target for the Hindu militants. The Rama Vivah, the day fixed for the beginning of the navah paath, was on 24 November 1949, but with so many vairagis and Hindu militants squatting on Muslim graves and igniting sacred fires there, it became impossible to hold back the crowd till the scheduled date.

The navah paath at the Ramachabutara, therefore, began on 22 November 1949, two days ahead of schedule,[29] under the aegis of the All India Ramayan Mahasabha. The campaign for the mobilization of Hindus was accelerated further. Wrote Akshay Brahmachari in his memorandum to Lal Bahadur Shastri, the home minister of the UP.

> Mass meetings were held. Loudspeakers fitted in *tongas* [horse-drawn carts] and cars kept screaming day in and day out, calling upon the people to come for *darshan* in the mosque where yajna [...] was taking place, as the place of Ram's birth was being reclaimed. People began coming in thousands also from outside the town in cars sent by the organizers of the show. Inflammatory speeches were made and it was openly announced that the Babri Masjid was to be converted into a Sri Rama Temple. Mahatma Gandhi, Congress and Congressmen were openly abused.[30]

Obviously, the navah paath was more an exercise in politics than in religion. As the show was managed by the Hindu Mahasabha through its proxy, the tone and tenor had to follow its political line. Akshay Brahmachari was quick to note this point:

> Developments taking place in Ayodhya and Faizabad and the question of Babri Mosque are neither a simple question of mosque or temple nor a fight between Hindus and Muslims. This is a serious conspiracy by reactionary forces who want to use it to kill the ideals of Mahatma Gandhi and win electoral battle by raising communal passion. Local officials have also participated in this conspiracy.[31]

Nevertheless, the navah paath had begun with a lot of promise to Hindu communalists, who expected the event to provide a breakthrough for their Ayodhya strategy. The Ramachabutara had become, for the first time in its history, the most talked-about place in Ayodhya. The Ramayan Mahasabha's promise of an imminent 'miracle' had created a sensation. Both Hindus and Muslims flocked to the site, the former to bear witness to the 'miracle' of Rama reclaiming his 'original place of birth', the latter to watch helplessly the siege of the Babri Masjid.

V

On 4 December 1949, the navah paath ended, but without being able to 'persuade' Lord Rama to leave the chabutara and 'shift' to his 'original place of birth' within the Babri Masjid. It was a big setback for the organizers. It was clear from the outset that they had to make the 'miracle' happen or lose for ever the confidence of the lay devotees who were unaware of the conspiracy and had poured into Ayodhya from all directions. Many among the organizers had thought that someone from the crowd, led by the heightened passion, would break into the mosque and install an idol there. If not from the crowd, they had expected someone from their own ranks to play Nathuram Godse in this case too. They were hoping to use that moment to declare that Rama had taken possession of his 'original place of birth'. They waited all those days for that to happen, especially after the atmosphere had been sufficiently poisoned. But none of that happened, not even during the extended period of the navah paath. For, while the navah paath had traditionally meant the recitation of the *Ramcharitmanas* continuously for nine days, the one that was held at the chabutara had lasted for thirteen days – four days more than the usual practice.

Not just ordinary Hindus, even vairagis were feeling let down. For, the devotees thronging the area in large numbers had expected to see a miracle. Such a colossal failure was certain to hurt the credibility of the organizers, particularly the vairagis of Hanumangarhi, where the decision for the navah paath had been taken. All eyes were now on the Ramayan Mahasabha and the vairagis. Bhaskar Das recalls:

> Everyone seemed utterly bewildered. No one seemed to know what to tell the devotees. Murmurs had begun and people had started saying that it was all a drama enacted for the sake of collecting offerings. It all seemed a crude joke. The resentment against the organizers of the navah paath was clearly visible.[32]

However, the leaders of the All India Ramayan Mahasabha – the acolytes of Mahant Digvijai Nath – were untroubled by these incendiary comments. Although disappointed about not being able to incite people enough to get things done on their own, they were not ready to give up. To them, the time was not over yet. The first thing they did was to organize bhandaras or religious feasts on a daily basis near the chabutara. The objective was to ensure that the dejected vairagis did not leave the place completely – a possibility that would have made the situation even more difficult. In Ayodhya, bhandaras, where free food is served, have always been a major attraction for vairagis. So it worked, and the vairagis, who had so enthusiastically captured the graveyard and participated in the navah paath and whose enthusiasm was now ebbing away, were held back for a good part of the day. Singing of kirtan continued at the chabutara, and dakshina was paid to all, be it a vairagi or a lay devotee, for participating in it.[33]

Once the Ramayan Mahasabha succeeded in ensuring the presence of a crowd at the chabutara for most part of the day, the backstage activities gained momentum. At the behest of the organizers of the navah paath, a group of Ramanandi sadhus met K.K.K. Nair to discuss the ways to break the deadlock. Prominent among the sadhus were Sitaram Das (gaddi-nashin or head of Hanumangarhi), Rampadarath Das (mahant of Vedanti Ashram, Janakighat, Ayodhya), Siakishori Saran (mahant of Hanumat Niwas, Swargdwar, Ayodhya), Ramsubhag Das (mahant of another temple in Swargdwar, Ayodhya) and Abhiram Das. This is what Satyendra Das had to say:

> There were some more sadhus in that meeting, but I don't remember their names now. They were of the opinion that the surreptitious

> planting of the idol of Rama Lalla would be much better than taking over the mosque through a mass action. Nair gave them the impression that he would provide all the possible help from behind the scenes if they planted the idol stealthily.[34]

This assurance by Nair was crucial, for it changed the entire scenario. The local leaders of the Ramayan Mahasabha as well as the section of vairagis working with them knew that they did not have to worry about the consequences, and that the local administration would rather cooperate with them than take stern action against them. It was indeed a promise that Nair and his assistant fulfilled when required, and they did so with deliberation and precision.

It was now just a question of finding a person suitable and willing to carry out the job of planting the idol stealthily, and of ensuring that suitable follow-up actions were taken so that the idol so placed was not removed. It took the leaders of the Ramayan Mahasabha about a week to resolve that issue, and the meeting – held on 21 December 1949, a day before Abhiram Das led his band of intruders into the mosque – that followed proved to be a critical turning point in the implementation of the Ayodhya strategy. The plan that was finalized in this meeting was carried out in the manner it had been visualized.

The venue of this meeting was a rather low-profile temple – called Jambwant Quila – located about two hundred paces away from Hanumangarhi. It was one of the innumerable temples that were constructed in Ayodhya by zamindars and businessmen of nearby areas during the late nineteenth and early twentieth centuries, and which were placed under the overall charge of Hanumangarhi. Jambwant Quila, in the Nazarbagh area of Ayodhya, was constructed in 1895.

The temple had a high fortress gate that covered a large elevated courtyard flanked by residential blocks, verandas, guest quarters and storerooms. In the centre of the courtyard was a huge havan kund covered by a tin shed resting on four wooden pillars while at the end of it stood a temple dedicated to Rama. Attached to the gate on the inner side was a chamber that contained a few wooden chairs and a table.

It was this chamber of Jambwant Quila that saw, on 21 December, the Hindu Mahasabhaites giving the final shape to their strategy and holding their last meeting before charging towards the Babri Masjid. The meeting was organized by, and was held under the presidentship of, the mahant of Jambwant Quila, Balram Das, the third mahant of this temple since it came up over fifty years ago. This is what Mahant Avadhram Das had to say about Balram Das:

> Mahant Balram Das was a chamatkari [manipulative] baba. He became mahant of Jambwant Quila in 1942 and remained so till his death in 1969. In December 1949, when everyone was clueless as to how to do this [installation of the idol in the mosque], the mahant called a meeting to take a collective decision on the issue.[35]

It was a meeting of selected people. Besides Balram Das, it was attended by K.K.K. Nair, as well as the local leaders of the Mahasabha – Gopal Singh Visharad, Ramchandra Das Paramhans and Abhiram Das.

It was decided that Abhiram Das and Paramhans, together with another vairagi – Vrindavan Das – would sneak into the Babri Masjid before midnight the next day (22 December 1949). The deadline was significant because that was the time when the duty of the guard – who had been persuaded to look the other way in the event of vairagis trying to sneak into the mosque – was to end at the gate of the Babri Masjid. Once inside the mosque, they were to lie low till around four in the morning, after which they were to light a lamp, chant mantras and beat the ghanta-ghariyal as loudly as they could.

Gopal Singh Visharad was given the responsibility of mobilizing Hindu devotees in large numbers – from Ayodhya as well as from nearby villages and townships – the very next morning and to arouse a lot of passion so that the local administration, even if under pressure from higher authorities, could fall back on the argument that the use of force might lead to large-scale loss of life and property.[36]

When Abhiram Das emerged from Jambwant Quila with Ramchandra Das Paramhans in tow he went straight to Ramghat. While Paramhans left for his residence, Abhiram Das walked further up to the temple where his brothers and cousins lived. This is what Awadh Kishore Jha remembers of the night:

> That evening there was a glow on the face of Abhiram Das. I was certain that he was up to something, but did not know exactly what it was. For the last few months he had been very busy and of late he had started looking tired. But that evening he seemed to have become rejuvenated. He kept talking to us and had his evening meal there only. However, he did not say anything about the plan.[37]

The following night, despite Paramhans backing out, Abhiram Das led his small band of intruders, scaled the wall of the Babri Masjid and jumped inside with a loud thud.

4

CHAPTER

Nehru–Patel Stand-off

THE SOUND OF A thud reverberated through the medieval precincts of the Babri Masjid like that of a powerful drum and jolted Muhammad Ismael,[1] the muezzin, out of his deep slumber. He sat up, confused and scared, since the course of events outside the mosque for the last couple of weeks had not been very reassuring. For a few moments, the muezzin waited, standing still in a dark corner of the mosque, studying the shadows the way a child stares at the box-front illustration of a jigsaw puzzle before trying to join the pieces together.

Never before had he seen such a dark cloud hovering over the mosque. He had not felt as frightened even in 1934, when the masjid was attacked and its domes damaged severely, one of them even developing a large hole. The mosque had then been rebuilt and renovated by the government. That time, it had been a mad crowd, enraged by rumours of the slaughter of a cow in the village of Shahjahanpur near Ayodhya on the occasion of Bakr-Id. This time, though the intruders were not as large in number, they looked much more ominous than the crowd fifteen years ago.

As the trespassers walked towards the mosque, the muezzin – short, stout and dark-complexioned, wearing his usual long kurta and a lungi – jumped out of the darkness. Before the adversaries could discover his presence, he dashed straight towards Abhiram Das, the vairagi who was holding the idol in his hands and leading the group of intruders. He grabbed Abhiram Das from behind and almost snatched the idol from him. But the sadhu quickly freed himself and, together with his friends, retaliated fiercely. Heavy blows began raining from all directions. Soon, the muezzin realized that he was no match for the men and that he alone would not be able to stop them.[2]

Muhammad Ismael then faded back into the darkness as unobtrusively as he had entered. Quietly, he managed to reach the outer courtyard and began running. He ran out of the mosque and kept running without thinking where he was going. Though he stumbled and hurt himself even more, the muezzin was unable to feel the pain that was seeping in through the bruises. Soon, he was soaked in blood that dripped at every move he made. He was too stunned to think of anything but the past, and simply did not know what to do, how to save the masjid, where to run. There was a time when he used to think that the vairagis who had tried to capture the graveyard and who had participated in the navah paath and kirtan thereafter had based their vision on a tragic misreading of history, and that good sense would prevail once the distrust between Hindus and Muslims – which had been heightened during Partition – got healed. That was what he thought during the entire build-up outside the Babri Masjid ever since the beginning of the navah paath on 22 November, and that was why he never really believed the rumour that the real purpose of the entire show in and around the Ramachabutara was to capture the mosque.

Muhammad Ismael had always had cordial relations with the priests of the Ramachabutara. The animosity that history had bequeathed them had never come in the way of their day-to-day interactions and the mutual help they extended to each other. Bhaskar Das – who was a junior priest of the small temple at the Ramachabutara in those days and who later became the mahant of the Nirmohi Akhara – also confirmed this.

> Before 22 December 1949, my guru Mahant Baldev Das had assigned my duty at the chabutara. I used to keep my essential clothes and utensils with me there. In the night and during afternoon, I used to sleep inside the Babri Masjid. The muezzin had asked me to remove my belongings during the time of namaz, and the rest of the time the mosque used to be our home.[3]

While the chabutara used to get offerings, enough for the sustenance of the priest there, the muezzin usually always faced a crisis as the contribution from his community for his upkeep was highly irregular. Often, vairagis, particularly the priest at the chabutara, would feed the muezzin.[4] It was like a single community living inside a religious complex. Communalists on both sides differentiated between the two, but, for the muezzin they were all one.

But it was not so once the vairagis entered the mosque that night. The trust that he had placed in them, he now tended to think, had never been anything but his foolish assumption. It had never been there at all. In a moment, the smokescreen of the benevolence of the vairagis had vanished. The muezzin seemed to have experienced an awakening in the middle of that cold night. His new, revised way of thinking told him that the men who had entered the Babri Masjid in the cover of darkness holding the idol of Rama Lalla had no mistaken vision of history. Indeed, these men had no vision of any kind; what they had done was a crime of the first order, and what they were trying to accomplish was simply disastrous.

Despite his waning strength, Muhammad Ismael trudged along for over two hours and stopped only at Paharganj Ghosiana, a village of Ghosi Muslims – a Muslim sub-caste of traditional cattle-rearers – in the outskirts of Faizabad. The residents of this village, in fact, were the first to awaken to the fact that the Babri Masjid had been breached when a frantic 'Ismael Saheb' came knocking on their doors at around 2 a.m. on 23 December 1949. Abdur Rahim, a regular at the mosque before it was defiled, had this to say:

> They might have killed Ismael saheb. But he somehow managed to flee from the Babri Masjid. He reached our village around 2 a.m.

> He was badly injured and completely shaken by the developments. Some villagers got up, gave him food and warm clothes. Later, he began working as a muezzin in the village mosque, and sincerely performed his role of cleaning the mosque and sounding azan for prayer five times a day until his death in the early 1980s.[5]

In Paharganj Ghosiana, Muhammad Ismael lived like a hermit. He could neither forget the horror of that night, nor overcome the shock that broke his heart. He was among the few witnesses to one of the most crucial moments in independent India's history, and the first victim to resist the act. Spending the rest of his life in anonymity, he appeared immersed deep in his own thoughts, mumbling, though rarely, mostly about 'those days'. Life for the trusting muezzin could never be the same.

II

That was it, then: after over four centuries of being in existence, the Babri Masjid, the three-domed marvel of Ayodhya, had fallen into the hands of a small band of intruders, and Hindu communalists of all shades had conspired to achieve this carefully woven key aspect of the Mahasabha's Ayodhya strategy. The involvement of K.K.K. Nair and Guru Dutt Singh, in particular, proved to be critical. For in those days, district magistrates used to be powerful figures in local administration, and city magistrates were among their more formidable administrative adjuncts.

With the two most significant officials in the district administration openly working for the conversion of the mosque into a temple, it was only to be expected that the officials under them would help the Hindu Mahasabha in whatever manner they could. The government enquiry that followed the surreptitious planting of the idol in the masjid ratifies this hypothesis. Though never made public for many reasons, the enquiry report revealed that the followers of K.K.K. Nair and Guru Dutt Singh used the authority which these two men commanded to persuade the police guarding the mosque to look the other way while Abhiram Das led his band of intruders carrying the idol of Rama.[6]

That the policeman guarding the Babri Masjid did play this role in seeing the conspiracy through was also hinted at by Bhaskar Das, the junior priest in the temple of Rama Lalla at the chabutara in 1949:

> At that time a guard was posted at the gate [of the Babri Masjid] because the Muslims had complained that the Hindus would try to capture the mosque. This complaint had been filed after the large-scale defiling of graves in the vicinity of the Babri Masjid. The police used to encourage us to capture the mosque and install the idol there ...[7]

That being the mood of the police, it would not have been too difficult for the Hindu communalists to take the guard into confidence – and there were various ways to do that – and persuade him to look the other way. On being asked as to what kind of help the guard provided to the intruders, Mahant Bhaskar Das laughed and said, 'It was all God's miracle. Till the time He wished to stay at the chabutara, He remained there, and when He decided to shift inside the mosque, He did that.'[8]

Yet the miracle, before it could happen, had to be adjusted with the duty hours of the guard who had been won over. It was for this reason that the idol of Rama had to be smuggled in before twelve in the night on 22 December 1949. For a Muslim guard – Abul Barkat – was to take charge after that. Abul Barkat, in a sense, was himself a victim of the police conspiracy hatched to ensure the success of the Mahasabha's plan. By the time Barkat resumed his duty at midnight that fateful night, the intruders had already gone inside with the idol of Ram Lalla along with a silver throne for the deity, the photographs of some other deities as well as various materials used for pooja and aarti. By twelve o'clock, the mosque had already been captured and the sole resistance capitulated after being brutally dealt with. For a few hours after capturing the mosque,

Abhiram Das and his gang lay low, not doing anything loud enough to make Abul Barkat suspicious. He was totally ignorant of the developments that had taken place behind his back. Recounted Indushekhar Jha:

> Abhiram Das sat just beneath the central dome of [the] Babri Masjid firmly holding the idol in his hands and we got active. We threw away all the articles [of previous possessors], including their urns, mats as well as clothes and utensils of the muezzin. We then erased many Islamic carvings with the help of a khurpi [a sharp-edged instrument generally used for gardening purposes] from the inner and outer walls of the mosque, and scribbled Sita and Rama in saffron and yellow colours on them.[9]

Around four in the morning, while it was still pitch dark, the intruders, following the script finalized in Jambwant Quila the day before, lit the lamp and started doing aarti. This must have frightened Abul Barkat who was completely unaware of the developments of the previous night, for it would now be impossible for him to explain as to what he was doing when the vairagis sneaked into the mosque. Dozing off or being away from the spot – even if he was not – while on his job to guard such a sensitive structure was an utmost dereliction of duty. Abul Barkat, therefore, must have been in a fix, and what he saw inside the mosque must have numbed him to the core. This predicament explains not just his inability to do anything that night but also his statement much later.

In the charge sheet filed on 1 February 1950, based on the FIR registered in the morning of 23 December 1949 against Abhiram Das and others for intruding into the mosque and defiling it, Abul Barkat was named as one of the nine prosecution witnesses. What he said in his statement to the magistrate elated the Hindu communalists, but any sane person could easily see through it. Justice Deoki Nandan in his 'Sri Rama Janma Bhumi: Historical and Legal Perspective' has cited a 'concise translation' of Abdul Barkat's statement:

> He [Abul Barkat] was on duty at the Police Outpost Rama Janma Bhumi on the night between December 22nd and 23rd, 1949. While on duty that night, he saw a flash of Divine Light inside the *Babari Masjid*. Gradually that light became golden and in that he saw the figure of a very beautiful godlike child of four or five years the like of which he had never before seen in his life. The sight sent him into a trance, and when he recovered his senses he found that the lock on the main gate (of the mosque) was lying broken and a huge crowd of Hindus had entered the building and were performing the *aarti* of the Idol placed on a *Singhasan* and reciting: *Bhaye prakat kripala Deen Dayala* [God has manifested himself].[10]

The Hindu Mahasabha and other communal organizations immediately lapped up Abul Barkat's statement as a proof of the 'miracle' that had happened on that fateful night when Lord Rama himself 'reclaimed' his 'original' place of birth. Decades later, however, even those who had propagated the miracle theory in order to prove their point were found laughing at it. Bhaskar Das, for example, said, 'What else could Abul Barkat say? When such an incident happened while he was on duty, he had no other option but to say what he was told to say in order to save himself.'[11]

Acharya Satyendra Das, one of the disciples of Abhiram Das who later became the chief priest of Ramajanmabhoomi, was no less straight in his observations:

> Abhiram Das and others had taken the idol of Rama Lalla inside the mosque well before twelve o'clock that night when the shift at the gate changed and Abul Barkat resumed his duty. And when after midnight and before dawn the beating of ghanta-gharial began along with the aarti he woke up and saw that scene. In his statement, he said what he saw thereafter.[12]

Abul Barkat could never explain his position. Perhaps the pressure of the district administration that had already gone communal and his own desperation to save his job at any cost never allowed him to come out of the darkness of that night.

III

It was indeed a strange night – full of surprises for some like Muhammad Ismael, the muezzin, and Abul Barkat, the guard, but not really so for others. The defilers of the mosque were not the only people for whom the night was progressing exactly in the manner it had been visualized. The president of the Faizabad unit of the All India Hindu Mahasabha, and the lieutenant of Mahant Digvijai Nath, was also aware of the uniqueness of the night.

Around the same time that Abhiram Das was leading his group inside the mosque, this man – Gopal Singh Visharad – was sitting in a printing press, trying to get as many posters and pamphlets printed as he could before dawn. These materials, which announced the 'miracle' of Rama Lalla reclaiming the Babri Masjid – even though the capture of the masjid had only just begun – and exhorted ordinary Hindus to throng in large numbers to the 'holy' spot, were to form the basis for the Mahasabha's massive mobilization drive the next morning.[13]

It was a small printing press, located in the Shringarhaat area of Ayodhya, about two kilometres away from the Babri Masjid, and was owned by one Brahmadev Shastri. Shastri had bought it in 1943 from someone belonging to Sultanpur district in UP and changed its name from 'Narayan Press' to 'Ramesh Art Press', in memory of his son who had died some time ago. Many years later, in 1958, Brahmadev Shastri was found murdered and his elder brother, who now started running the press, renamed it 'Brahmadev Printing Press'.[14]

In 1949, Brahmadev Shastri was a good friend of Gopal Singh Visharad. He was also very close to some of the vairagis of Hanumangarhi. A prominent Hindi weekly, called *Virakta*, which had a pronounced Hindu communal bias and which was being edited by a known Mahasabhaite, Ramgopal Pandey 'Sharad', was printed in Shastri's press. In fact, weeks after the planting of the idol, the Criminal Investigation Department (CID) had raided the office of Ramgopal Pandey, as well as the premises of Brahmadev Shastri's press as it suspected their role in the printing of the provocative pamphlet in Hindi that had been distributed among people during the navah paath at the Ramachabutara. The pamphlet, which did not carry the mandatory print line, was titled 'Jaichand Aur Mir Zafar Ke Ye Bete' [These Sons of Jaichand and Mir Zafar][15] and was an attack on those defending the rights of Muslims.

Such was Brahmadev Shastri's association with the Mahasabha and Hanumangarhi that his press used to get most of its printing orders from them. Nothing unusual was therefore happening on the night of 22 December 1949 when Gopal Singh Visharad sat in the press till late, eager to get the printing completed before dawn.

For Visharad, this was a very hectic and equally uncertain night. He was aware that it was uncertain for Abhiram Das too. The first time they met was in 1946, in one of the political events of the All India Hindu Mahasabha, and they had often seen each other during the subsequent years, but they got to know each other only in Faizabad Jail. That was the time when Mahasabhaites all over the country were being rounded up following the assassination of Mahatma Gandhi. Abhiram Das was arrested a few days after Gopal Singh Visharad was picked up from his Sringarhaat residence in February 1948. Both were, however, released in May 1948.

The two came out of prison as great friends. While Abhiram Das was very loquacious and often foul-mouthed, Visharad was generally an introvert, but a sharp, observant man. Again, while Abhiram Das was almost illiterate and could barely write his name, Gopal Singh Visharad was well educated, the term 'Visharad' itself being a literary honorific in Hindi equivalent to graduation in the English system of education. Physically, too, they were quite apart – while Abhiram Das was a giant, Visharad was considerably short in height and looked even shorter as he walked with his friend. But none of these differences could affect their friendship. The ideology the two men shared outweighed their differences.

For some time after being released, the two friends had lain low, remaining busy with their respective work. Visharad's shop, 'Bundelkhand General Stores', the main source of his livelihood, had been closed. While Visharad was in jail, the assistant, who was his country cousin, had burgled it and run away with all the goods stocked in the shop.[16] For the next few months, therefore, he remained preoccupied with finding new sources of livelihood for his family.

But once the Mahasabha decided to resume its political work and started regrouping itself, Visharad was his old self again. As general secretary of the All India Ramayan Mahasabha, his engagement with the naga vairagis of Hanumangarhi increased manifold as soon as the preparations for the celebration of Hanuman Janmotsava began. In all this, he was ably assisted by Abhiram Das. There was another factor that kept the duo together and on the same track. Both sought – and received – guidance from Mahant Digvijai Nath, who had now started taking more interest in the affairs of Ayodhya than ever before.

For three months before the night of 22 December 1949, Gopal Singh Visharad was so busy that he was seldom at home. Abhiram Das too was constantly in and out of Hanumangarhi during this period. Equally occupied all these months was their third friend, Ramchandra Das Paramhans, the president of the city unit of the Mahasabha and joint secretary of the All India Ramayan Mahasabha. And with Mahant Digvijai Nath closing in on Ayodhya, minutely observing each development there, there was no rest for them at all.

To Visharad, therefore, the night of 22 December 1949 must have appeared to be the climax of a very hectic process. It must have been the same for Abhiram Das. As Visharad did not meet him after dusk that evening, he was hardly likely to know that their third friend, Ramchandra Das Paramhans, had dropped out of the plan at the last minute and disappeared from the scene, leaving Abhiram Das in the lurch, at least for a while.

Yet, the plan did not falter, and the night began, unsure whether it would ever meet dawn.

IV

The night appeared equally prolonged to Awadh Kishore Jha. The dramatic appearance of Abhiram Das at his Ramghat Temple residence around eleven that night and his even more dramatic departure a few minutes later left him so bewildered that Awadh Kishore could not sleep a wink. Like his elder brothers Yugal Kishore Jha and Indushekhar Jha, he too wanted to follow Abhiram Das, but his brothers stopped him, saying it was too late for him to go out. As a younger brother, he had no option but to obey his elders. This is what he recounted later:

> Around five o'clock in the morning [of 23 December 1949] I left the bed and started running like a mad boy. Within a few minutes I reached the Janmabhoomi. It was still dark, but I did not have much patience after what Abhiram Das had said at night and the way he had left the Ramghat temple. From the bustle of the previous few days, I could make out that it was something to do with the Babri Masjid, but I did not know exactly what they were up to.[17]

What Awadh Kishore, who was sixteen at that time, saw then was something unexpected:

> When I reached, it was quiet everywhere. The flickering light of a lamp was visible inside the mosque. I went closer and saw Abhiram Das sitting on the floor, tightly holding the idol of Rama Lalla in his hands. Beside him were three or four sadhus, as well as Indu Babu [Indushekhar Jha] and Yugal Babu [Yugal Kishore Jha]. At a little distance was [K.K.K.] Nair. When I moved closer, I heard Nair Saheb telling Abhiram Das: 'Maharaj, don't move from here. Don't leave Rama Lalla alone. Tell everybody to raise the slogan that Rama Lalla is hungry.' I still remember that scene. Nair Saheb looked firm and serious.[18]

As Awadh Kishore described the scene in detail, it became clear that by five that morning, K.K.K. Nair was in full control of the mosque.

In his interaction with Abhiram Das and other vairagis, he looked like the authority which had to be obeyed – hand on hip, leaning forward, making his point with a belligerent finger.

That was significant. The district magistrate of Faizabad was among the first to reach the spot once Abhiram Das finished the operation successfully in the dead of the night. At that time the masjid only had a handful of people and Ayodhya was asleep. No one would have known about the incident – or people would have come to know so late that no commotion would have been possible – had the district magistrate acted swiftly and removed the idol and images of Hindu deities from the mosque and scratched away the writings, not many in number, from its inner and outer walls. So, he could have easily restored the mosque's status quo ante without creating any fuss among Hindu believers. That was also expected of any district magistrate anywhere in the country.

But it was not a normal situation, and the district magistrate of Faizabad was not acting innocently; he was more interested complicating the problem than resolving it. He therefore wanted to delay the official response to the development that had taken place the previous night. For he knew that the official note of the incident would not take much time to go beyond Faizabad and reach Lucknow and even Delhi. But he wanted the news to reach Lucknow officially only after he had ensured the irreversibility of the conversion of the masjid into a temple. He wanted the crowds to swarm into Ayodhya from all around to witness the 'miraculous appearance' of Rama Lalla before officially taking note of the incident. The weight of numbers and strength of popular belief, Nair was certain, would act like bulwarks against any attempt by Lucknow or Delhi to reverse what had happened in Ayodhya.

It was for this reason that the FIR of the incident was lodged only at nine in the morning though Nair had reached the spot at five. It took the district magistrate an hour and a half more to send a brief radio message to the premier of the United Provinces, Govind Ballabh Pant, as well as to the state's chief secretary and home secretary. The radio message that was sent at 10.30 that morning said:

> A few Hindus entered [the] Babari Masjid at night when the Masjid was deserted and installed a deity there. DM [District Magistrate] and SP [Superintendent of Police] and force at spot. Situation under control. Police picket of 15 persons was on duty at night but did not apparently act.[19]

It was a shrewd message which spoke about the dereliction of duty of the 'police picket of 15 persons' which was placed much away from the mosque – in fact, outside the complex itself – but remained silent about the guard who had been on duty at the gate of the inner courtyard of the mosque ever since the local Muslims expressed their apprehension about Hindus trying to grab their place of worship. Also, Nair had put the best possible gloss on an incident that had the potential to shake the nation. His message gave the impression – contrary to the reality – that the situation was under control and that senior district officials had reached the spot.

That Nair was determined to delay the official response to the problem was clear even in the testimony of Akshay Brahmachari, the secretary of the Faizabad District Congress, who fought against the takeover of the mosque right from the beginning:

> On the 23rd morning the District Magistrate told me at about 9 a.m. that the image of Ram Chandraji was implanted in the Babari Masjid the preceding night, and that he had learnt of the incident at 6 a.m. from Sri Bhai Lal and that he had gone to see it. It passes all comprehension as to how Bhai Lal could know of the incident so early that morning and could inform the District Magistrate while the police guards of the mosque did not know about it. The District Magistrate did not even care to know as to how Bhai Lal could know all about it so early in the morning. It has to be particularly remembered that the District Magistrate quoted Bhai Lal for many such informations.[20]

Akshay Brahmachari believed that there was no one called Bhai Lal and that it was a fictitious character invented by Nair to carry out his agenda smoothly without getting dragged into any controversy. Perhaps Brahmachari was right. For, in no official records nor in any interview with the elders of Ayodhya and Faizabad could a man named Bhai Lal be traced. At the most, it might have been the nickname of somebody quite close to, or perhaps an insider of, Hindu communal organizations like the All India Hindu Mahasabha or the RSS.

V

As time passed, it became clear that K.K.K. Nair had succeeded in his efforts. The crucial moments that could have been used to undo the damage that was likely to result from the outrageous act had passed. Gradually, narrow streams of devotees began moving towards the Babri Masjid. Without much delay, these streams started widening until they took the form of a deluge pouring in from all directions to witness the 'miracle' that had happened the night before.

Presenting itself as the All India Ramayan Mahasabha, the All India Hindu Mahasabha was skilfully overseeing the mobilization of Hindu devotees from Ayodhya as well as from surrounding rural areas. Pamphlets announcing the 'miracle' of Rama Lalla 'reclaiming' his 'place of birth' had already been printed and Mahasabhaites got into action without wasting a moment. Akshay Brahmachari, in his memorandum to Lal Bahadur Shastri, the home minister of the United Provinces, observed:

> From that very morning loudspeakers started announcing the appearance of *Bhagwan*, exhorting all Hindus to come for *darshan*. Tension went on increasing. Notices and handbills continued to be distributed. Thousands of people started pouring in for *darshan* into the city in cars and public carriers sent out from Faizabad. Inflammatory speeches were made before them saying that the

Congress was destroying Hinduism, that since there was not a single temple left in Pakistan, they should join together to root out all signs of Muslims from Ayodhya, which could be possible only if the Congress was rooted out. It was also said that most of the Congressmen subscribed to these views, but Jawaharlal Nehru and a few others were siding with the Muslims.'[21]

There was reason for the Hindu militants to believe that Congress members subscribed to those views. For, the Mahasabhaites were not the only ones campaigning against the move to restore the mosque back to Muslims. Some Congress members too were seen publicly supporting the Mahasabhaite campaign, as was pointed out by Akshay Brahmachari in his memorandum to Lal Bahadur Shastri:

> Even Congress leaders like Vishwanath Dayal Tripathi and Raghav Das lost their balance and publicly supported the cause of the reactionaries in their speeches. They said that [...] democracy meant the will of the majority, and since the majority of the people obviously do not like the mosque, it could not be restored. If the government interfered in the matter, they would resign from their seats in the Assembly. They claimed to be speaking in a representative capacity and they said that they spoke with the fullest sense of responsibility.[22]

Nehru couldn't agree more with Brahmachari and noted how Baba Raghav Das had supported the capture of the Babri Masjid once it fell into the hands of Hindu communalists, as also the growing communalization of the Congress party in the United Provinces.

Nevertheless, by the afternoon of 23 December, huge crowds converged on Babri Masjid. But Hindus were not the only ones getting attracted to the 'miracle'; a large number of Muslims also descended there as the news reached them that their place of worship had been defiled and captured by Hindus. Recounted Awadh Kishore Jha:

> At one point, Muslims seemed to be gearing up to launch a massive attack to liberate the mosque. That frightened Abhiram Das, who

> was holding the idol of Rama Lalla and sitting just beneath the middle dome of the Babri Masjid. In panic, he looked up towards Nair. But before Abhiram Das could say anything, Nair shouted at him, 'Ai buddhe, baithe raho, bhaga to goli mar denge' [Hey old man, keep sitting; If you move, I will shoot you].[23]

Somehow no major communal clash took place that day. Meanwhile, as Hindus and Muslims continued to throng the mosque, the tension kept growing, and the situation threatened to escalate into a major communal flare-up. For Nair, the circumstances had become much more problematic than he had ever expected. The chief secretary of the United Provinces, Bhagwan Sahay, and the inspector general of police, V.N. Lahiri, were sending frantic messages to Faizabad that the idol and other paraphernalia be removed from the Babri Masjid. On its part, the state government had come under heavy pressure as the developments in the temple town had infuriated Nehru.

Not only was Nair faced with what appeared to be an insurmountable pressure from above, the ground beneath him started trembling as well. Ayodhya seemed to have become a veritable tinderbox ready to explode any moment. A full-fledged riot was staring the district magistrate right in the face. It was clear that the distance he had travelled so far in promoting the cause of Hindu communalists was no match for the challenges lying ahead. Even a minor mistake at this juncture had the potential to take away all the gains the Hindu militants had made in Ayodhya so far. Capturing the mosque was one thing, but retaining it forever was something else. One part of the conspiracy had ended, the other just begun. In the first part, Nair had the luxury of anonymity as he was operating from behind, but in the second part, he had become the centre of the storm.

To brave the storm, the first thing Nair did was to ensure that a section of Hindus continued to celebrate the 'miracle' on a regular basis outside the Babri Masjid, near the entrance of the inner courtyard. His wife, Shakuntala Nair, proved instrumental in this, while the mobilization part was taken care of by Mahasabhaites and vairagis. It was largely at her behest that on 23 December 1949, some sadhus organized an akhand kirtan and chanting of devotional songs near the gate of the mosque.[24] It was a ploy to permanently deploy a strong contingent of Hindu militants at the doorstep of the mosque, so that removing the idol became extremely difficult even during odd hours.

Nair now turned his attention towards the pressure emanating from Lucknow. In his first detailed letter to the chief secretary, Bhagwan Sahay, dated 26 December 1949, Nair strongly defended his own case, stressing that at no point did he have any reason to suspect that Abhiram Das would actually instal the idol inside the mosque, nor, he further argued, did he have any grounds to take action against leaders like Raghav Das. Significantly, he referred only to Raghav Das – the Congress leader aligned in the whole exercise with the Hindu Mahasabha – quietly ignoring the names of non-Congress Hindu communalist leaders. This was a shrewd move to throw the ball in the court of Congress, the party that governed the province as well as the Centre. He wrote:

> [...] Abhiram Das, the sadhu who headed the small crowd which was responsible for this act, is neither a Mahant nor in any sense a leader. His name did not even come to prominent notice in this connection. The speeches made by leaders including Baba Raghava Das never advocated violence and were not actionable. There was therefore no question of our taking any steps either to arrest the leaders or to start any proceedings against them. And in any case the arrest of the leaders, in my view, could not have prevented this mischief by a small body of persons who depend on immense public sympathy in support of this cause. While the arrests would not have prevented this crisis, they could conceivably have precipitated the tension in some form.
>
> The mosque can be entered only through the temple premises and is so accessible at all times. Further, the temple premises are occupied at all hours. And the mosque is deserted all the time except for one hour during Friday prayers. To prevent determined Hindus from getting into the mosque either by force or in secret, the

> mosque would have to be permanently policed with a force which must cost the exchequer thousands of rupees a month. Although this controversy led to many riots in the past thirty-six years [...] and tremendous holocausts in lives, I do not believe that there was any decision to police the mosque permanently. Surely, if permanent policing was a remedy, [the] government, who could not have been unaware of the controversy that has raged for centuries over this and other disputed shrines in the province, would not have failed to provide [a] permanent police force for this purpose. And in the absence of any such arrangement, the local authorities [...] could not have made out a case before [the] government for the policing of a deserted and almost unused mosque permanently at a tremendous cost to the tax-payer.
>
> [...] Now that this incident has happened at Ayodhya, [the] government could think of policing this and other similar disputed shrines, such as those in Benaras, Mathura, etc., on a permanent basis, to prevent such mischief. And if the government does not decide to do so, would the district authorities be held responsible for any future mischief in these places of however unexpected or unsuspected a character[?][25]

In the same letter, Nair, having made all arrangements to secure a victory for Hindu communalists, emphatically declined to carry out any order to remove the idol from the mosque:

> Why the idol is not removed, and why it was not removed on 23rd morning, are facile questions to ask. The removing of the idol by force is possible, though at some cost with the police force now available. Removal surreptitiously at night against weaker resistance is also possible. But that such removal without consideration of consequences would in my view have been a step of administrative bankruptcy and tyranny. The short-term reactions on public tranquillity can be guarded against with the force now available though it was not possible on 23rd with our limited resources. Even now I doubt if we can do much, if communal riot flares up in places remote from headquarters [...] I fully believe that the solution must be found without tremendous cost [to] life and property [...]

> I would therefore emphasize that the question of removing the idol is not one which the Superintendent of Police and I can agree with or carry out on our initiative. The alternative solution which I have proposed to the government has a fair chance of success in preserving peace and policy. If this solution is not accepted and if [the] government decides to remove the idol and face the consequences, then it is only fair that I, having lost [the] government's confidence in this matter, and being of the view that the solution dictated to me is neither correct, necessary, advisable nor legally justifiable, should not be asked to put it into effect. I would, if [the] government decided to remove the idol at any cost, request that I be relieved and replaced by an officer who may be able to see in that solution a merit which I cannot discern [...][26]

Meanwhile, K.K.K. Nair, together with his assistant Guru Datt Singh, had also been trying hard to push the crisis into a legal impasse so that there would be a legal bar on removing the idol from the mosque. Getting a property declared disputed and attaching it under Section 145 of the Criminal Procedure Code (CrPC), 1898, was not very difficult for district magistrates those days. Nair could easily have done that with the help of his subordinates in the local administration. The only issue, therefore, was identifying an amenable person for the post of the receiver for this attached property. With the groundswell of passion only increasing among both the communities, Nair wanted to complete the exercise sooner than later. It was for this purpose that Nair and Singh sought help from Babu Priyadatta Ram, the chairman of the Faizabad-cum-Ayodhya Municipal Board.

Babu Priyadatta Ram referred to this issue in an interview that he gave to Harold A. Gould, the author of *Grassroots Politics in India*. As per Gould, the chairman of the municipal board claimed that Nair and Singh begged him to intervene as the situation had gone out of their control and they were alarmed at the way things had actually turned out. Although it would be difficult to ascertain what really transpired between Priyadatta Ram and the two civil servants, it is clear that the municipal board chairman did provide help to Nair and Singh in a manner they wanted him to. Gould wrote:

> In a state of near panic, the two [Nair and Singh] went late one night to Babu Priyadatta Ram[...] and begged him to intervene [...] Priyadatta Ram succeeded in devising a formula which saved the Pant government from embarrassment, saved the careers of the two erstwhile politically ambitious civil servants, and guaranteed that any further confrontations between the Hindu and Muslim communities over the Babari Masjid would at least be delayed [...][27]

The decision to rope in Priyadatta Ram for the purpose was a shrewd tactical move. He was, at that time, the best choice as he was capable enough to establish contact with all parties engaged in the dispute and, at the same time, deal quietly with the state government. Moreover, as the subsequent developments proved, his inclination, like that of Nair and Singh, was also towards Hindu communalists. Being the third generation of his family to lead the Kayastha Party, a strong caste party in Faizabad, he commanded a wide local network which could be deployed deftly at the service of K.K.K. Nair and Hindu communalists.

Having devised a foolproof plan to keep the communal cauldron in Ayodhya boiling, Nair once again shifted his attention towards Lucknow, this time to scuttle the state government's proposed move to get the idol removed from the Babri Masjid. On 27 December 1949, a day after his first letter, he shot off a second one to Bhagwan Sahay, the chief secretary of the UP government. This letter, written in response to Faizabad commissioner Shyam Sundarlal Dar's order to remove the idol from the mosque, was much bolder than the previous one, and Nair, confident of settling the issue in favour of Hindu communalists, refused to carry out the order, arguing that it would rekindle communal violence:

> The Commissioner returned from Lucknow and gave me and the Superintendent [of] Police the outline of a scheme for removing

the idol from the mosque surreptitiously to janmabhumi temple outside the mosque. The scheme was discussed yesterday before [the] Commissioner, I.G., D.I.G. (P.A.C.), S.P. and myself. It was discussed again this morning by all of us.

The idea of the removal of the idol is not one which I can agree with or wish to carry out on my initiative for it is fraught with the gravest danger to public peace over the entire district and must lead to a conflagration, of horror unprecedented in the annals of this controversy. The district is aflame and it is reported that licence-holders for firearms have promised support with their arms in a fight against police and officers if it becomes necessary. It will be no easy or quick matter to collect arms from all licensees in [the] district to prevent such a sanguinary outcome. The Hindus, with no exception that I know of, are behind the demand for keeping the idol *in situ*, however disunited they may be on the propriety of the act which led to [the] present situation, and are ready to kill and die in [sic] this cause. The depth of feeling behind the movement and the desperate nature of the resolves and vows in support of it should not be underestimated or pooh-poohed. When the storm breaks out, it may be possible to quell riots within municipal limits with the force at our disposal, but firing will have to be resorted to in certainty and many lives will be lost not only from the firing but also in the repercussive fulminations over the entire district. Today rumour is rife that the removal of the idol is being contemplated and Hindus are reported to have decided to attack Muslim habitations [...] It will not be possible to protect the lives of the Muslims in all places if the storm breaks out [...] I have so far failed to find any Hindu even among Congressmen who is ready to support the move for [the] removal of the idol.

[...] I shall also be unable to find in the district a Hindu, let alone a qualified priest, who will be prepared on any inducement to undertake the removal of the idol. Kripal Singh (the S.P.) and I are at our wits-end [sic] to find a person who could do this for us if it becomes necessary. No person in the district is likely to be ready for this errand, for his life and property will thereafter be forfeit in the eyes of the entire Hindu population. We suggested that Commissioner, I.G. and D.I.G. help us by getting a man from outside

> who would be able to do this as our resources are limited in this district in which the situation excludes all hopes of success in our quest. But they could not agree to find us the necessary instrument and I doubt if [the] government themselves could find us a suitable one, if our resources failed. Further, any attempt on our part to approach a qualified priest is likely to give away the move, if the priest refuses, as he most certainly would. And if the removal is carried out anyhow through anybody, the storm of indignation [...] will spread beyond the confines of the district.[28]

In this letter, Nair also proposed in unambiguous language that the Babri Masjid be attached and turned into a temple. He wrote:

> [The] [g]overnment, must, I earnestly request, listen to my voice and accept that any attempt to adopt a solution involving the use of force in the present state of intense and desperate feeling is bound to lead to terrible happenings. [...]
>
> The question now remains as to what is to be done in the present situation. The installation of the idol in the mosque has certainly been an illegal act, and it has placed not only local authorities but also [the] government in a false position. We have to see how the position can be resolved as far as possible without such terrible cost and sacrifice. I have a solution to offer for the government's consideration.
>
> The mosque would be attached and both Hindus and Muslims should be excluded from it with the exception of the minimum number of *pujaris* – I am attempting to reduce the numbers of *pujaris* from three to one without creating another impasse – who would offer *pooja* and *bhog* before the idol which could continue. The *pujari* or *pujaris* will be appointed by order of the magistrate. The parties will be referred to the Civil Court for adjudication of rights. No attempt will be made to hand over possession to the Muslims until the Civil Court, if at all, decrees the claim in their favour ...[29]

In the meantime, Nair got into action to entangle the issue in a legal web. A crucial one week was allowed to pass before the proceedings under Section 145 of the CrPC, 1898, were drawn up *suo motu* by

Magistrate Markandey Singh, and a preliminary order was issued on 29 December 1949 attaching the Babri Masjid and appointing Babu Priyadatta Ram as its receiver. With Lucknow not acting to carry out its resolve to restore the mosque to Muslims, Priyadatta Ram took charge of the disputed property on 5 January 1950 and submitted to the district magistrate a scheme of arrangements necessary for the upkeep and worship of the idol installed in the mosque.

Nair had succeeded. The mosque had been turned into a temple. A few months later, he and Guru Datt Singh were removed from their posts. In 1952, Nair's wife became a member of Parliament from Gonda on an All India Hindu Mahasabha ticket and, in 1967, Nair himself won a Lok Sabha election from Bahraich on a ticket from the Jana Sangh, an offshoot of the Mahasabha. Guru Datt Singh also entered politics and continued to play a prominent role in the communal politics of Faizabad for some time.

VI

If K.K.K. Nair sought to bluff Lucknow, the premier of the province, Govind Ballabh Pant, did not do better in his dealings with the Centre, particularly Jawaharlal Nehru. The news of the desecration of the Babri Masjid by Hindu communalists and the district administration's unwillingness to undo the wrong committed on the night between 22 and 23 December 1949 did not take much time in filtering through to Delhi. Nehru was quick to respond. On 26 December, he sent a telegram to Pant:

> I am disturbed at developments at Ayodhya. Earnestly hope you will personally interest yourself in this matter. Dangerous example being set there which will have bad consequences.[30]

For a while after this telegram, it appeared that the state government was really serious about restoring the mosque to Muslims. Indeed, pressure was exerted on the district administration to get the

The 'asan' of Abhiram Das, the prime accused in the planting of the Rama idol inside the Babri Masjid

A rare photograph of Abhiram Das, taken just before his death

Indushekhar Jha was one of the two cousins who followed Abhiram Das into the Babri Masjid on the night of 22 December 1949

Abhiram Das's youngest brother Upendranath Mishra was in Ayodhya, and living with Abhiram Das in December 1949

Dharam Das, Abhiram Das's youngest disciple, who inherited his asan; he is holding the walking staff once used by Abhiram Das

Abhiram Das's cousin Awadh Kishore Jha was one of the first to reach the Babri Masjid on the morning of 23 December

Gopal Singh Visharad filed a petition in the civil court of Faizabad, obtaining an injunction against the removal of the Rama idol

Baba Raghav Das, a vital cog in the Hindu Mahasabha's conspiracy

Guru Datt Singh, the city magistrate of Faizabad and a supporter of K.K.K. Nair

A young Digvijai Nath

Digvijai Nath (second from right), one of the prime accused in the Mahatma Gandhi murder case, was also crucially involved in the conspiracy to take over the Babri Masjid

Jambwant Quila, where the final crucial meeting was held to finalize the details of the Ayodhya strategy

Akshay Brahmachari with his long-time companion Meera Behn in their youth

Akshay Brahmachari and Meera Behn

Akshay Brahmachari with Babu Jagjivan Ram

Akshay Brahmachari (second from left) greeting
Lal Bahadur Shastri (extreme right)

The Gandhian Akshay Brahmachari, who struggled relentlessly against the grand conspiracy of the Hindu fundamentalists

idol removed. But once K.K.K. Nair refused to carry out the order given to him, Lucknow did not do much to implement Nehru's instructions. Precious time was lost in the name of 'exploring all avenues' and soon it was too late. Pant wrote to Nehru on 4 January 1950:

> Ayodhya affairs are still causing a lot of worry. We are in touch with the prominent citizens and Congressmen of Faizabad and Ayodhya [...] We are exploring all avenues in order to find a satisfactory solution in a peaceful way. We are anxious to do justice without resorting to methods that may lead to still greater excitement or other serious consequences. The situation is delicate but not hopeless. I need not say more in this letter, but as I have wired to you, Lal Bahadur will see you personally whenever it suits your convenience.[31]

But Nehru was aware how the delay had the potential to turn this apparently localized affair into an all-India problem. He expressed his concern in his letter to Pant dated 6 January 1950. Pant telephoned him the same day and told him that he wanted 'some well-known Hindus' to persuade the people of Ayodhya before he could take any action. Nehru talked about the delay tactics of Pant in his letter to C. Rajagopalachari, the last Governor General of India, which he wrote on 7 January, the very next day:

> I wrote to Pantji last night about Ayodhya and sent this letter with a person who was going to Lucknow. Pantji telephoned me later. He said he was very worried and he was personally looking into this matter. He intended taking action, but he wanted to get some well known Hindus to explain the situation to people in Ayodhya first.[32]

Nehru was getting restive. Despite Govind Ballabh Pant's repeated assurances that efforts were being made to set things right, nothing seemed to be happening on the ground. For Nehru, the developments in Ayodhya were a matter of grave concern and he offered, if necessary, to go to Ayodhya himself. He wrote to Pant on 5 February 1950:

> I shall be glad if you will keep me informed of the Ayodhya situation. As you know, I attach great importance to it and to its repercussions on all-India affairs and more especially Kashmir. I suggested to you when you were here last that, if necessary, I would go to Ayodhya. If you think this should be done, I shall try to find the date, although I am terribly busy.[33]

Pant, however, dissuaded Nehru from proceeding to Ayodhya, assuring him that K.K.K. Nair and Guru Datt Singh had been replaced and that he was expecting some satisfactory solution to be found and the idol of Rama removed peacefully. This, Pant wrote in his letter dated 9 February 1950:

> Jai Kirat Singh, who was acting as Chief Commissioner of Rampur, has been placed in special charge of Faizabad and Ayodhya as Additional Commissioner. He is an experienced, tactful and dependable officer and will faithfully carry out the instructions given to him. The City Magistrate of Ayodhya has already been replaced by another officer. District Magistrate Nayyar [sic] will also be transferred shortly. Certain precautions had to be taken before removing him from Ayodhya. He is erratic and obstinate. Jai Kirat Singh is at the head of the affairs now and Nayyar [sic] has been relegated to the background. But he should have no official connection with Ayodhya. We propose to appoint another Collector in his place very soon. The situation continues to be delicate and complicated, though there is no local excitement over it now [...] I am aware of the importance of the subject and of the concern and embarrassment that it has been causing to you. I would have myself requested you to visit Ayodhya if the time were ripe for it. I shall do so if necessary at the appropriate moment. For the present, I think, I need not encroach upon your valuable time for this purpose when, besides your other engagements, you have to attend the Parliament and cannot conveniently leave Delhi.[34]

It was obvious that Pant was playing his own politics on the issue. He himself had set the communal tone during the by-elections of

1948 and his protégé, Baba Raghav Das, was openly issuing threats that he would resign from the Legislative Assembly if the idol was removed from the mosque. Relying heavily on the 'Hindu vote', he could hardly have been expected to do much to annoy Hindus, especially in the Ayodhya–Faizabad region that had helped him become the sole master of the party unit in UP.

Pant was, at the same time, aware that Nehru could not do much so long as he (Pant) enjoyed the confidence of Sardar Vallabhbhai Patel, a supporter of Hindu chauvinism in the Congress. By the time the Babri Masjid was taken over by Hindu communalists, the Pant–Patel axis had developed deep roots in the Congress. Thus, even though Patel – the home minister and deputy prime minister of India – wrote to Pant to find a peaceful solution to the Ayodhya problem, on no occasion did his tone develop an edge against the premier of UP. In a letter to Pant on 9 January 1950, Patel wrote:

> The Prime Minister has already sent to you a telegram expressing his concern over the developments in Ayodhya. I spoke to you about it in Lucknow. I feel that the controversy has been raised at a most inopportune time [...] So far as Muslims are concerned, they are just settling down to their new loyalties [...] I feel that the issue is one which should be resolved amicably in a spirit of mutual tolerance and goodwill between the two communities. I realize there is a great deal of sentiment behind the move which has taken place. At the same time, such matters can only be resolved peacefully if we take the willing consent of the Muslim community with us. There can be no question of resolving such disputes by force.[35]

Pant could not have expected a better letter from Patel. In his reply on 13 January 1950, the premier of UP expressed his gratefulness:

> Whenever in difficulty, I look up to you. You are always so kind and generous and an unfailing source of strength and light in moment[s] of gloom and depression. When I recall all that had happened here in your presence I feel deeply mortified. It may have given you an idea of the agony that I have to undergo almost from day to day ... I

> have to thank you for your letter about [the] Ayodhya affair. It will be of great help to us here. Efforts to set matters right in a peaceful manner are still continuing and there is a reasonable chance of success, but things are still in a fluid state and it will be hazardous to say more at this stage.[36]

It was many months later – after all talk of removing the idol had subsided and court proceedings had taken over all other debates – that Govind Ballabh Pant made his position on the Babri Masjid clear. On 18 October 1950, he sent 'a narrative prepared by the Home Secretary'[37] (of UP) on the affairs in Ayodhya as desired by Patel. The 'narrative' gave the same argument as had been used by K.K.K. Nair – that since it was not possible to remove the idol without using force, the mosque was 'attached' on 29 December and the chairman of the local municipal board was made in-charge of it. In the 'narrative', the home secretary also reproduced an extract from the *District Gazetteer* of Faizabad, according to which Babur, who visited Ayodhya in 1528 and halted there for a week, 'destroyed the ancient temple and on its site built a mosque, still known as Babur's mosque'.

Nehru had, however, begun to suspect the intentions of Pant. His delaying tactics and his dilly-dallying on restoring the occupancy of the Babri Masjid left Nehru utterly frustrated. Moreover, Pant's casual approach towards this crucial issue left no doubt in Nehru's mind that Pant was more determined to keep the problem in Ayodhya alive. In his letter to Pant on 17 April 1950, Nehru was unequivocal in his expression of this frustration:

> I have not been to the U.P. for a long time. That is partly due to lack of time, but the real reason is that I hesitate to go there. I do not wish to come into conflict with my old colleagues and I feel terribly uncomfortable there, because I find that communalism has invaded the minds and hearts of those who were the pillars of the Congress in the past. It is a creeping paralysis and the patient does not even realize it. All that occurred in Ayodhya [...] was bad enough. But the worst feature of it was that such things should take place

> and be approved by some of our own people and that they should continue.
>
> It seems to me that for some reason or other or perhaps [due to] mere political expediency, we have been far too lenient with this disease that has been spreading all over India and now in our own province. Sometimes I feel that I should leave everything and take up this matter only. Perhaps some day I shall do that. If I do it, it will be a crusade with all the strength that I possess.[38]

And then on 18 May 1950, he wrote in his letter to Dr Bidhan Chandra Roy, the chief minister of West Bengal:

> In Ayodhya an old mosque built by Babur was taken possession of by a mob led by *Pandas* and *Sanatanists* of the place and I regret to say that the U.P. Government showed great weakness in handling the situation.[39]

Nehru, however, had to wait for some more time before he could start his crusade.

5

CHAPTER

The Conspiracy Deepens

THE CALCUTTA SESSION OF the All India Hindu Mahasabha that began on 24 December 1949 was agog with news of the developments in Ayodhya, where, even then, the party's wing, the All India Ramayan Mahasabha was busy mobilizing Hindus to reinforce their occupancy of the mosque. Indeed, the moblilization was quite massive, for it provided K.K.K. Nair – the district magistrate of Faizabad who was now overtly a part of their camp – the necessary argument that any move to remove the idol from the Babri Masjid would lead to a massive loss of life and property in and around Ayodhya.

The Ayodhya development was significant not just because of the capture of the mosque, but also due to the Mahasabha's successful deployment of a large number of Hindus, for several days, on as communal an issue as converting a mosque into a temple. The event showed the delegates and leaders attending the conference that they were back in the reckoning, since it was the first mobilization on such a grand scale by the Mahasabha after the assassination of Mahatma Gandhi.

As in Ayodhya, so too in Delhi, three days before the murder of Gandhi, the mobilization had been done clandestinely. The then deputy superintendent of Delhi Police, Jaswant Singh, had told the

Kapur Commission inquiring into the conspiracy to murder the Mahatma that

> the Inspector in-charge of Parliament Street Police Station had told him that there was no information about the meeting and he heard about it at 4.30 p.m. and reached the place with a guard and on inquiry the Hindu Mahasabha people said that they had obtained permission of the District Magistrate which was later found to be incorrect. As the meeting was in progress and [a] large [...] audience was present, it was considered inadvisable to disperse the meeting; hence no action was taken.[1]

In Ayodhya, the massive mobilization of Hindus – first to 'persuade' Rama to perform the 'miracle' and then to witness the 'miracle' – was, therefore, a significant milestone in the revival of the Mahasabha. Yet, for the leaders of the Hindu communal outfit, the work still remained unfinished. It was just the beginning. Ayodhya represented a local climax, but that had to be magnified enormously. Only then could it pave the way for a grand revival of the party, in the UP and, if possible, in many more provinces of the country.

It became clear that the Hindu Mahasabha had taken a huge leap. The party that had been almost fully immobilized following the assassination of Mahatma Gandhi seemed to have suddenly stood up with a firm resolve and, during its annual conference, it decided to stage a political comeback. On 25 December 1949, on the second day of the three-day conference, the newly elected president of the Hindu Mahasabha, N.B. Khare, announced that the party was 'now re-entering the field of politics with the ideology of a cultural state of Hindu Rashtra after a temporary suspension of its political activities'. He further said:

> The pro-Muslim Congress has always ridiculed the Mahasabha as a communal organization. The Mahasabha has, at every stage, fought against the Congress' surrender to communalism. [...] We should forget all this [the clampdown on the Mahasabha following the assassination of Mahatma Gandhi] as a bad dream. We harbour no

> ill feelings against the government [...] The Congress, by insisting upon a secular state, wants to convert the Indian nation into irreligion and materialism, the causes of the moral rot. If this rot is to be stopped, the ideology of a secular state must be given up and the ideology of a cultural state must be adopted. Hindus being 85 per cent of the population, their culture would be the culture of the state or Rashtra. Congress leaders say they would not allow the establishment of a Hindu Rashtra in this country; nobody wants Hindu Raj or Hindu government. Their confusion must stop. Hindu Rashtra is already there, and no power on earth can destroy it.[2]

Khare wanted to make this speech on 24 December, the very first day of the conference, right after his election as the president of the Mahasabha and after V.D. Savarkar had delivered his inaugural address. But he could not do so because the session on the first day had to end abruptly following the failure of the sound system at the venue. Many years later, Khare, elaborating further on his views with regard to the irreconcilable differences between Hindus and Muslims in the country, said:

> In almost everything we [Hindus and Muslims] represent the opposites, the contrary points of view. For example, it is like this: our *choti* [tuft of hair kept on the head by a devout Hindu] points to heaven, the Muslim's *dadhi* [beard] points towards *patal* [hell]; we pray facing the east, they pray facing the west; we begin our writing from the left side, they begin their writing from the right side; we burn our dead, they bury them. Thus, there are far too many basic fundamental differences between the two cultures.[3]

N.B. Khare's strange understanding of Indian culture led him to arrive at dangerous conclusions:

> It is my firm belief that to solve the problem of this nation there should be a change of constitution. Muslims should be regarded as second class citizens. They should be allowed freedom of movement everywhere. They should be permitted to enter trade or commerce; practice [sic] their culture; their money, property should

> be protected. But they should stay away from politics. They should not be permitted any part in the political life of the country. That change should be made in the constitution. Unless that is done, this country cannot progress. This will always be a land of conflict.[4]

With such a man as the president of the Hindu Mahasabha, the message at the Calcutta conference of the party was unequivocally clear – rabid communalism, and nothing else, would be the party's guiding star. Ayodhya could not have happened at a more opportune time. The party realized that it must consolidate the gains it had made in the temple town.

II

The consolidation began at different levels. The Calcutta conference ended on 26 December 1949 with a huge rally of party workers and supporters. The new office-bearers of the party took about a week's time to settle down. In Ayodhya too the immediate aftermath of the installation of the idol was marked by open and vehement attempts by local Mahasabha leaders and by K.K.K. Nair to deflect all moves to shift it out.

As soon as the local leaders cleared the pitch, the central leadership of the Mahasabha jumped in to take up the Babri Masjid–Ramajanmabhoomi issue as a means to mobilize the conservative and communal sections of Hindus nationwide. On 8 January 1950, V.G. Deshpande, the national vice-president of the party, wrote a letter to Tej Narain, the working president of the United Provincial Hindu Mahasabha, and Bishan Chandra Seth, general secretary of the party's state unit, asking them to accompany him to Ayodhya:

> I am reaching Ayodhya on the 15th [of] January in connection with the Ram Janmabhoomi dispute. I will let you know the exact train and time of my arrival there. I hope you would kindly accompany me to Ayodhya and also intimate the same to the Hindu Mahasabha people and all others concerned there.[5]

The same day, Deshpande wrote another letter, this one to Gopal Singh Visharad:

> I am coming to Ayodhya and Faizabad on the 15th [of] January 1950 to see with my own eyes the situation existing there and see what can be done with regard to Ram Janmabhoomi. I would let you know the exact time and train of my arrival telegraphically. You are also requested to be in touch with Sri Tej Narayan ...[6]

Deshpande reached Ayodhya one day late. On 15 January, he arrived in Lucknow where, at the railway station, he was received by Tej Narain. Deshpande spent most of that day in discussions with Tej Narain and Bishan Chandra Seth on ways to turn the developments in Ayodhya into a national issue. Also present at the meeting was the provincial party unit's secretary-in-charge of propaganda, Vishwanath Agrawal.

The next morning, Deshpande, Tej Narain and Agrawal left for Ayodhya. They got down at Faizabad Railway Station. Mahant Digvijai Nath also arrived from Gorakhpur in his car. The leaders thereafter addressed a massive public meeting organized by the Mahasabha outside the railway station, from where they proceeded in Digvijai Nath's car towards Ayodhya. Among those who greeted the Hindu Mahasabha leaders on the outskirts of Ayodhya was Ramchandra Das Paramhans, who had gone back to his usual routine. In fact, after scooting from the scene on 22 December 1949, Paramhans had handled his situation quite deftly. As the meeting at Jambwant Quila was a secret and no one let out anything about the installation of the idol, so that the 'miracle' could be established, Paramhans had no trouble resurfacing merely days afterwards. This he did as quietly as when he had left the scene. In all the chaos and excitement prevailing in Ayodhya, no one noticed his exit or return. Even those who were aware of Paramhans's disappearance at the nick of time were no longer interested in raking up the issue. For, it was in the interest of none – at least at that point – to come out and discuss their deeds openly. That would have been deeply damaging to the Mahasabha.

The reception group led by Ramchandra Das Paramhans to welcome V.G. Deshpande in Ayodhya was moderate in size, and many of the people present were holding the Hindu Mahasabha flag. From there, Deshpande was driven through masses lining both sides of the street, shouting pro-temple and pro-Mahasabha slogans. Indeed, the mass base of the party had swelled enormously in the last few weeks in the district. One of the key factors was the fact that the conversion of the mosque into a temple had had a unifying effect on various groups of Hindu conservatives and communalists in Ayodhya. Not only were Baba Raghav Das and the majority of Congress members in the district with the Mahasabha, the Arya Samaj – a socio-religious organization founded in 1875 primarily to maintain the basic elements of the traditional social order and culture of the Hindus – also decided to close its ranks with Savarkar's party on the Babri Masjid–Ramajanmabhoomi issue.

It was this closing of ranks that led the Faizabad unit of the Arya Samaj – in the immediate aftermath of the desecration of the mosque by Mahasabhaites – to call upon the government to desist from restoring the masjid to Muslims. It, in fact, raised the pitch further, demanding that all temples which were said to have been converted by Mughals and other Muslim rulers into mosques be immediately handed over to Hindus all over the country. According to *Leader*, the English daily from Allahabad,

> The local Arya Samaj, at a meeting held on Sunday [25 December 1949] morning, resolved that all Hindu religious institutions in India which had been damaged and converted into masjids should be restored to the Hindus for being used for the purpose for which they were originally meant. The Samaj further resolved that the aforesaid policy be also observed in respect of Janam Bhoomi Temple at Ayodhya.[7]

To V.G. Deshpande, it was an opportunity full of immense possibilities. He visited the Babri Masjid, which had now been converted into a temple, talked to various sections of Hindus, including his own partymen, Arya Samajis and vairagis, and took copious notes.

One person who was not present in the group of Mahasabha leaders in Ayodhya on 16 January 1950 was Gopal Singh Visharad. All through the day, this central figure of the local party unit remained occupied in filing a suit in the civil court of Faizabad, seeking the issue of an order allowing him the right to worship the deity installed in the masjid while restraining the defendants from removing the idol.

In his suit, Visharad claimed that he was 'ill recently' and when he went to offer his 'prayers' at the 'Ram Janam Bhumi' after recovering from 'illness on 14 January 1950' the provincial government 'and its employees stopped me from entering the place where the idols of Shri Bhagwan Ramchandra and other gods are situated'. The suit further claimed that the provincial government had deprived Hindus of their 'legitimate rights of worship' and that it was 'exercising undue pressure on Hindus through its employees ... to remove the idols of Shri Bhagwan Ramchandra and other Gods from their present places'.

Gopal Singh Visharad, therefore, prayed for an order that he be 'entitled to worship and visit without obstruction or disturbance Shri Bhagwan Ramchandra and others' and that 'a perpetual injunction restraining the defendants from removing the idols' be issued.

Among the eight defendants listed in the suit, five were Muslims and the rest were state government officials, Deputy Commissioner K.K.K. Nair, Superintendent of Police Ram Kirpal Singh and Additional City Magistrate Markandey Singh.[8]

Acting on the suit, the civil judge directed the issue of a notice to the defendants, and in the meantime ordered, on the same day, the issue of an interim injunction as requested.[9]

The day of V.G. Deshpande's visit to Ayodhya was, therefore, a crucial one in the implementation of the Mahasabha's game plan. For, it was on 16 January that the party made the first serious move to consolidate its gains of 22 December 1949, both legally and politically. The interim injunction that Visharad obtained from the civil court was to become the bedrock upon which the politics of independent India would be turned around in the years to come.

III

When V.G. Deshpande left Ayodhya, he was driven by a new confidence. The Babri Masjid–Ramajanmabhoomi tangle appeared to be an effective way of enlarging the Mahasabha's base enormously. He was aware that the careful use and manipulation of this symbol could give his party a massive advantage over the Congress, particularly among the religious community it claimed to represent. Such a manipulation could unleash a miracle for the Mahasabha – one that the party had miserably failed to generate in the aftermath of the assassination of Mahatma Gandhi.

In Ayodhya, V.G. Deshpande had a long conversation with Mahant Digvijai Nath about the future course of action to capitalize on their latest communal aggression. Thereafter, while Digvijai Nath left for Gorakhpur, Deshpande proceeded to Varanasi.

Before leaving Ayodhya, the top leaders of the Mahasabha formed a local committee specifically targeted at addressing the problems related to the Babri Masjid and also opened a propaganda office in Faizabad under the leadership of Tej Narain, the working president of the United Provincial Hindu Mahasabha. It was planned that this office, with the help of the All India Hindu Mahasabha, would organize a countrywide campaign as part of which lakhs of letters, telegrams, resolutions and applications would be sent from all over the country to the central and provincial governments against any attempt to shift the idol.[10]

On 18 January, immediately after reaching Varanasi, Deshpande wrote a long letter to R.A. Kanitkar, the office secretary at the Hindu Mahasabha headquarters in New Delhi, and gave him proper instructions on how to go about converting the Ayodhya issue into a plank for the nationwide mobilization of Hindus. Based on this letter, the head office of the Mahasabha issued a circular to all its party units to observe 27 March 1950, the festival celebrating the birth of Lord Rama, called Rama Navami, as 'Rama Janmabhoomi Day'. The circular said:

> You may have learnt through papers the history of the real state of affairs about the Rama Janmabhoomi episode at Ayodhya. I am giving below a short note prepared by Sri V.G. Deshpande on this episode. You are hereby directed to observe 27th of March 1950 as 'Rama Janmabhoomi Day'. Lord Rama's birth-day falls on this day and hence on this day, public meetings should be held in all villages and towns in your province and a resolution demanding the retention of the Rama Janmabhoomi shrine with the Hindus should be passed and forwarded to U.P. and Central Governments.
>
> Attempts should be made to contact all the authorities of the temples in your town particularly Shree Ram temples and institutions like Arya Samaj, Arya Prathinidhi Sabha, Sanatan Dharma Prathinidi Sabha, Dharam Sangh, R.S.S., Varnashram Swarajya Sangh and Gurudwara Prabandhak Committee. All should be requested to conduct special prayers for retention of this shrine, where Lord Rama was born, with the Hindus, and be asked to tell the congregation which assembles for celebrating the birthday of Shree Ramachandra regarding the episode. The congregations in the temple should also be requested to pass similar resolutions.
>
> It is hoped that this matter will be given urgent attention and every attempt will be made to see that the day becomes a success.
>
> Arrangements for the publicity should also be properly made and reports of the observance of the day should be sent to the Head Office here.
>
> In addition to passing of resolutions and holding of meetings, pamphlets and posters on this issue should be issued in your respective localities.[11]

The Hindu Mahasabha hoped to gain substantially in the wake of this agitation since Rama is one of the most venerated gods in north India. The circular was accompanied by a personal note by Deshpande, exhorting Hindus all over the country to rise in support of the 'brave fight' being put up by 'the Hindus of Ayodhya' for the retention of what he called a Hindu shrine.

Interestingly, neither in the circular nor in the personal note of Deshpande did the Mahasabha utter a single word on what had happened on the night of 22 December 1949. Hiding this crucial fact was a shrewd political device to whip up passion on the basis of distorted information. The personal note of V.G. Deshpande attached to the party's circular said:

> At Ayodhya, there is an ancient shrine called 'Rama Janma Bhoomi' at the spot believed to be Shree Ramachandra's birth place and therefore a place of pilgrimage for Hindus. The temple constructed on the spot was a beautiful structure, built long ago, but now partially destroyed by Muslim fanatic rulers [...] The District Magistrate of Faizabad has posted police and even military near the place and it is feared that the attempt to remove the images may be made by the government. The shrine deserves to be declared a national monument and served as the birth-place of Shree Ram, the first Aryan hero, and the aggressive spirit of the Muslims deserves to be put down severely by the government and not allowed any indulgence. The Hindus of Ayodhya are putting up a brave fight for retention of the shrine. The Secretary of the Ayodhya Hindu Sabha has filed a suit for declaration of the right to worship at the shrine by Hindus and for injunction against removal of the images and against obstruction in their worship. Hindus all over India must represent to the U.P. and Bharat [Indian] Governments not to attempt the removal of the images and thus alienate the Hindu feeling throughout Bharat [India]. The U.P. Hindu Sabha has opened an office at Faizabad to prevent untoward incidents and to lead the movement to a successful end and deserves help from Hindus throughout Bharat [India].[12]

The Mahasabha, thus, sought to build an all-India movement centring on Ayodhya, launching a massive communal propaganda wherever the party had a presence. On the face of it, the objective was to foil all attempts to displace the idol from the Babri Masjid, but mixed with that was the opportunity to reap huge political dividends from the campaign.

IV

If the developments in Ayodhya lifted the spirits of the central leadership of the Mahasabha, they did so for the Hindu militants of Faizabad as well. Within weeks of appropriating the mosque, the Mahasabha opened a full-fledged office in Ayodhya. So far, the party, despite having a following in Ayodhya, lacked any formal office to take care of the day-to-day organizational and political activities there. The Arya Samaj, which possessed considerable amount of immovable property in Ayodhya, played a big role in getting the Mahasabha an office in the temple town.

Though the founder of the Arya Samaj, Dayanand Saraswati, was not a proponent of Hindu nationalism, and its members, up to the beginning of the twentieth century, viewed Hinduism as a degraded form of the Vedic religion, the ideological characteristics of this socio-religious organization were such that it became the crucible of Hindu nationalism in the last two to three decades of colonial rule. It, therefore, did not take much time for the Arya Samaj in Ayodhya to align itself with the Hindu Mahasabha once the latter raised the communal pitch. Kedarnath Arya, one of the most prominent Arya Samajis in Faizabad, now became an enthusiastic and generous sympathizer of Hindu militancy. It was primarily because of his efforts that the Mahasabha now had an office in Ayodhya.

Arya also became closely associated with the management of the akhand kirtan outside the Babri Masjid, as well as with the efforts to keep the vairagis of different akharas together. Yet, the question of control over the new janmabhoomi inside the Babri Masjid – which had eclipsed the old one at the chabutara – had begun to be fiercely debated among vairagis. All through, the Ramachabutara, the janmabhoomi till not too long ago, had remained under the control of the Nirmohi Akhara, but the installation of the Rama idol had been spearheaded by Abhiram Das, a vairagi belonging to the Nirvani Akhara. So, the infighting between the prominent akharas of the Ramanandi sect began as soon as it appeared the government had been forced to desist from removing the idol from the mosque.

None of the Mahasabha pointsmen in Ayodhya, however, was in a position to make the akharas patch up their differences. Gopal Singh Visharad was much too busy with his suit to be able to divert his attention towards the infighting among the vairagis, while Ramchandra Das Paramhans, despite being a vairagi himself, could hardly be expected to be taken seriously by these nagas as he belonged to the third akhara of the Ramanandi sect – the Digambari Akhara. Abhiram Das – who had by now become popular as Janmabhoomi Uddharak – was himself party to this fight and had, in fact, now begun calling himself the mahant of janmabhoomi.

With no one being able to manage the dispute, the situation soon threatened to go out of control. Kedarnath Arya, therefore, sent a letter to Mahant Digvijai Nath on 29 January 1950, informing him about the infighting among vairagis and the opening of the Hindu Mahasabha office in Ayodhya:

> Some differences have cropped up among *vairagis* at [the] *Janmabhumi*. In Ayodhya we have opened a Hindu Mahasabha office. I need to discuss with you something very urgent related to [the] Ayodhya issue. So please be at home on Sunday and confirm this to me over telephone of Raja Mohan Raja Bahadur. In Faizabad, he has got a telephone connection [...] I hope you will spare your valuable time for me.[13]

Mahant Digvijai Nath tried to settle the issue between the warring akharas, but he could not do much as none of the parties was ready to relent. Control over janmabhoomi meant control over all the offerings and donations that poured in. Neither akhara, therefore, wanted to give up its claim. Unable to resolve the issue, Mahant Digvaijai Nath gradually withdrew from the management of the janmabhoomi and began concentrating on using the symbol to stir up passions instead.

By this time, V.G. Deshpande had discussed with the mahant the plan to celebrate that year's Rama Navami festival – due on 27 March – as 'Rama Janmabhoomi Day'. Digvijai Nath, therefore, instructed Bishan Chandra Seth to make it a grand show in the United Provinces. The entire party got into an exercise to get maximum political advantage out of the festival that year. Nath also asked Seth to prepare a printed appeal for this occasion. After getting the appeal ready, Seth wrote to Digvijai Nath on 27 February 1950:

> As you told me on phone, I have prepared an appeal with regard to Rama Janmabhumi, and I am sending you a copy for your perusal. I have spent a lot of time on preparation of this appeal, which seems to have come out well. However, I will get it printed only after you have cleared it and informed your views to me through telegraph. Please also let me know as to how many thousands of copies of this appeal you want me to get printed.
>
> I must also inform you that I have already spent quite a lot of money on this. You will have to send me some money. Otherwise it will be difficult for me to get the appeal printed.[14]

The appeal did come out in printed form and was widely circulated on the day of Rama Navami. Perhaps Mahant Digvijai Nath did not delay in sending 'some money' to Bishan Chandra Seth.

Around the same time, Mahant Digvijai Nath was also preparing a booklet detailing the 'contributions' of the Mahasabha in 'persuading' Rama Lalla to shift his position away from the chabutara and reclaim his 'original place of birth'. Apparently, Gopal Singh Visharad was taking time in sending the crucial details for the booklet planned by the mahant. On 11 March 1950, therefore, Digvijai Nath wrote a rather terse letter to Visharad:

> I have reached here [Gorakhpur] in the morning today. Very soon a booklet on the issue of Rama *Janmabhumi* is being published from here. For this, we immediately require your photograph as well as the photograph of the *pandal* [at the janmabhoomi]. The *pandal* should be photographed from the side that has our party's board on it. Do it fast [...] Send other literatures [sic] also. Please don't delay in sending information related to all the developments there to the central [party] office, so that these could be [distributed] on time. I hope you will appreciate the urgency and do the needful immediately.[15]

Days before the Rama Navami that year, everyone in the Mahasabha, particularly in the United Provinces, seemed hyperactive – and terribly worried – as they did not want to miss the opportunity. The occasion had to be used to the hilt, and Hindus gathered even in the remotest corners of the province. No delay, no failure could be tolerated this time; all had to work in tandem. It was for this reason that when the party's head office in Delhi delayed the dispatch of the Ramajanmabhoomi propaganda material that was to be distributed on Rama Navami, Tej Narain, working president of the party's UP unit, chided Bhim Appa, one of the office-bearers at the headquarters. 'Ram Janmabhumi pamphlets should be ready before 27th March 1950, and you should send some to my address. Send some Shri Ram Janmabhumi receipts as well,' Tej Narain said in his letter.[16]

The Rama Navami that year was celebrated differently in many parts of the country, particularly in the United Provinces. The symbol of the janmabhoomi was sought to be built up. The mobilization was impressive in many temples. Appeals were distributed and political speeches made. The Hindu Mahasabha seemed to be finally got going and its message appeared to have started spreading among Hindus.

All this was encouraging for the Mahasabha leaders whose spirits had been lifted considerably. Sometimes this even blinded them. For example, on one occasion, months later, the party president,

N.B. Khare, came to an unusual conclusion. On 3 October 1950, a day after inaugurating the state conference of the UP Mahasabha at Moradabad, he issued a statement:

> I am glad that I came to Moradabad to inaugurate the Uttar Pradesh Hindu Sabha Conference. All the arrangements were very good and the attendance also was very large. The most significant thing which I observed was that on the 2nd [of] October 1950 on the [sic] Gandhi Jayanti Day, the Hindu Mahasabha meeting was attended by at least 20 thousand people. The Gandhi Jayanti meeting was attended by about 200 people. This is a definite indication that the influence of Gandhiism is declining among the masses which, according to me, is a very good sign for the ideology of Hindu Rashtra.[17]

Khare's optimism was unusual, but then he was known for his strange analyses and equally strange conclusions.[18] Yet, his optimism was mirrored by many Hindu communalists, especially in UP. To such people, it seemed to be a time to take a great leap forward.

V

Several years after K.K.K. Nair was relieved of his government job on 14 March 1950 – by which time he had established himself as a lawyer and shifted his residence to Lucknow – he told his attorney, Sadhu Saran Mishra, who looked after his property-related cases in the civil court of Faizabad, that there indeed had been 'proper planning' in which he and Guru Datt Singh played the role of 'initiators' while 'Thakur' Bir Singh, the civil judge of Faizabad, was the 'collaborator':

> It was done through a proper planning. Guru Datt Singh and I were the initiators and the civil judge was collaborator. We were apprehensive that even if we did something, the court might stay

> it. That time Thakur Bir Singh was the civil judge of Faizabad. One day we met the civil judge, told him about our planning and sought his cooperation in it. He said he would certainly like to cooperate as it was being done for the sake of Lord Rama, but the entire thing would have to be done within the limits of the law.[19]

It was an odd sort of confession, and certainly not an apology. That K.K.K. Nair and Guru Datt Singh played a major role in the incident is a well-established fact. Both government as well as independent researchers have concluded that the duo's role was too flagrant to be ignored on almost all counts, starting from the planning to the execution of the plot. Yet it is also true that these civil servants and innumerable Hindu communalists could not have succeeded in their mission, and the illegal possession of the mosque would have been reversed had the local judiciary acted differently.

Even a cursory glance at the way the criminal case, which was initiated after the filing of the FIR on 23 December 1949, was allowed to lose its way or the manner in which Section 145 of the Criminal Procedure Code of 1898 was interpreted leaves only one impression – that the Babri Masjid fell victim to not just a political conspiracy but a judicial one as well.

Nair's claim of judge Bir Singh playing the role of a 'collaborator', despite the latter's insistence on doing the 'entire thing' under the 'limits of the law', therefore, assumes immense significance. For it was the 'limits of the law' that were crossed once the crime was committed on the night of 22 December 1949. The case was straight and the legal provisions for such situations unambiguous. Had the law been followed, there would have been summary remedy against the forced occupation of the mosque, and the aggressor would have been asked to prove his claim in a regular civil suit against the party originally in possession. But that was not done, and what *was* was a glaring crossing of the 'limits of law'.

Sordid means were applied to take over the Muslim place of worship and the penal provisions invoked in the FIR included Section 147 (for rioting), Section 295 (for defiling the place of worship) and Section 448 (for trespassing) of the Indian Penal Code.

The charge sheet filed on 1 February 1950 named Abhiram Das the main accused in the case. No investigation was undertaken to probe the role of Mahasabha leaders in this act. The case lingered for a few years but eventually got submerged under the civil suits that had been filed by the local Hindu Mahasabha leaders. On 18 August 1953, a local Hindi weekly, *Virakta*, carried a report based on the order, dated 30 July 1953, of the city magistrate, Faizabad, Prem Shankar. The report, titled 'Janmabhoomi Ki Shaandaar Vijay [Glorious Victory of Janmabhoomi]', said, 'The honourable judge [...] has ordered that the case be closed for the lack of evidence and Baba Abhiram Das be acquitted of the charges [of planting the idol in the mosque and desecrating it].'[20]

However, before the charge sheet was filed on 1 February 1950, the case had taken a different turn. This became possible simply because Section 145 of the Criminal Procedure Code of 1898 was used not to reverse the act of wrongful dispossession but rather to sanctify it. Section 145 empowers the magistrate to ask the parties to file their claims, not on the title to the property, but 'as respects the fact of actual possession of the subject of dispute'. The magistrate decides 'which of the parties was' in possession. If a party has been 'forcibly or wrongfully dispossessed', the magistrate may treat it as if it had been in possession. It is then restored in possession, leaving it to the aggressor to file a civil suit to establish his title to the property.[21]

This crucial aspect of Section 145 was deliberately ignored during the course of the proceedings drawn up *suo motu* by Magistrate Markandey Singh. The subversion of this law began on 29 December 1949 when a preliminary order was issued attaching the mosque and appointing the chairman of the municipal board of Faizabad-cum-Ayodhya, Babu Priyadatta Ram, as its receiver. That very day, the order was pasted outside the Babri Masjid as well as the Ayodhya Police Station and sent for publication – together with K.K.K. Nair's covering letter – to *Leader*, the English daily in

Allahabad, and two local weeklies, one in Urdu and the other in Hindi. *Virakt*, the Hindi weekly that received the order, published in its subsequent issue:

> I, Markandey Singh, magistrate, first class, and additional city magistrate, Faizabad-cum-Ayodhya, after being fully satisfied by information received from police sources and from other credible sources that a dispute between Hindus and Muslims of Ayodhya over the question of rights of proprietorship and worship in the building claimed variously as Babri Masjid and Janmabhoomi Mandir, Mohalla Ram Kot, within the local limits of my jurisdiction, is likely to lead to a breach of the peace [...] the station officer of Ayodhya Police Station is ordered to attach the said property immediately and present it in the receivership of Sri Priyadatta Ram, chairman, Faizabad-cum-Ayodhya Municipal Board. He will be the receiver of the property in dispute and arrange for its management.[22]

Priyadatta Ram assumed charge on 5 January 1950. The scheme that he proposed to Nair for the management of 'the premises in dispute' turned Section 145 upside down. The scheme said:

> In compliance of a proper order duly served on me I assumed charge on the 5th of January 1950, of the premises in dispute in the Janmabhumi, Ajodhia, which were attached under Section 145. I am required to submit a scheme of its management. The most important item of management is the maintenance of the *bhog* [offering to deity] and *puja* [worship] in the condition in which it was carried on when I took over charge.
>
> The number of *pujaris* [priests] cannot be less than three. Two persons are required to keep constant watch to prevent the depredations of monkeys who snatch away the flowers from the *singhasan* [the throne carrying the idol of Rama] and lift away other things.
>
> Below I give the various *bhogs* which are being performed, the items of which they consist, and their daily cost [...]
>
> In addition to this staff mentioned above there should be a supervisor at Rs 45 to look to all these things.

The three *pujaris* will be getting food in the form of *bhog*. The head *pujari* will get Rs 15 p.m. and other two Rs 5 p.m. each. There will be a *kaher* also who will be getting Rs 30 p.m.

This brings the total expenditure on the maintenance of the premises to Rs 1057 p.m.

On the income side we have the cash offerings only [...]

The watch and ward arrangement of the premises will continue as here before, i.e. by the police. The entry of the portion in the dispute area will also be regulated as before. The *pujaris*, my local representative and other persons employed by me should be allowed free access.

I await your instructions about funds.

The Magistrate in charge should be intimated about this.[23]

The district magistrate promptly approved the scheme of management submitted by Priyadatta Ram. Thus, the mosque was turned into a temple and placed in the custody of the municipality, and the litigation was allowed to take its course.

The receiver's scheme had a basic flaw. It simply overlooked the 'forcible and wrongful dispossession' as evident from the FIR, filed not even a fortnight back. The FIR clearly said, '... a group of 50–60 persons had entered the Babri Masjid after breaking the compound gate lock of the mosque or through jumping across the walls [of the compound] with a ladder and established therein, an idol of Shri Bhagwan and painted Sita Ram, etc. on the outer and inner walls. [...]'[24]

Thus, the spirit of Section 145 was killed, and the Babri Masjid declared a 'property in dispute' which was likely to 'lead to a breach of the peace'. The party that had been dispossessed on 22–23 December 1949 was completely excluded, and the mosque was allowed to pass into the hands of Hindu communalist mobs.

Weeks later, the civil judge of Faizabad, Bir Singh, did not have any need to cross the 'limits of the law'. Acting on a petition filed by Gopal Singh Visharad, he issued an injunction – first on 16 January and then on 19 January 1950 – restraining the removal of the idol from the Babri Masjid and anyone from interfering with the puja carried on therein since 23 December 1949. 'The opposition parties are hereby restrained by means of a temporary injunction to refrain from removing the idols in question from the site in dispute and from interfering with *puja*, etc. as at present carried on ...'[25]

No one from among the dispossessed came forward to resist it, just as no one from their side had come forward to file an FIR. Even the muezzin wept silently, and died in the course of time with an invisible wound that kept festering all his life. No one asked why none among the Muslims came out to stake the community's claim over their place of worship, for no one could claim that the answer was still unknown, or that fear was not all-pervasive in the community.

Ayodhya had rolled into darkness. The night seemed permanent, dawn nowhere in sight.

6

CHAPTER

A Gandhian's Lone Stand

K.K. NAIR PRESIDED OVER Faizabad for nine months and fourteen days, from 1 June 1949 till 14 March 1950 when he was relieved of his job, and in that short period, he made a huge impression – most of them through a series of conspiracies – in the district. The mutilation of the mosque was just one testimony to his conspiracies; almost all others involved his insatiable appetite for amassing huge chunks of land in and around Faizabad for himself.

Nair's greed tended to blind him. Like a true communalist, to whom religion matters only so long as it can be used for non-religious and highly selfish purposes, Nair did not hesitate to grab even the land donated in the name of God. In this, opium became his weapon and the Ranopali Nanakshahi Temple – one of the oldest temples of the Udaseen sect – his victim.

The Ranopali Nanakshahi Temple, located in the outskirts of Ayodhya, is the main ashram of the Udaseen sect. According to tradition, this sect was founded in the seventeenth century by Shri Chand – the eldest of the two sons of Guru Nanak, the founder of Sikhism. The Udaseens are, therefore, also known as Nanakputras, the sons of Nanak, and they revere the Granth Saheb, the sacred book of the Sikhs. Later, on being excommunicated by the successors of Guru Nanak, they gradually turned to Hinduism. By and large, they started functioning as an independent order and was greatly influenced by Shaiva sanyasis. There is a belief that a Shaiva sanyasi, Bhakta Giri, was the first to be initiated by Shri Chand. So, like Shaiva sanyasis, the Udaseens worship dhuni and adhere to Shankaracharya's philosophy of advaita or absolute non-dualism. In other respects, too, they closely resemble Shaiva sanyasis, and are usually attired in red or black clothes, apply ashes and have long, matted hair. Their pantheon consists of five deities called panchayatana – Shiva, Vishnu, the Sun, Goddess Durga and Ganesh – besides their founder Guru Shri Chand.

In 1949, the Ranopali Nanakshahi Temple controlled huge tracts of fertile agricultural land that was acquired mostly through donations from the nawabs of Awadh. Nawab Asaf-ud-Daullah (1775–97) had, for example, donated a plot of one thousand standard bigha,[1] at the centre of which this temple was built. It also controlled thousands of bighas on the other side of the Sarayu in nearby Basti (now part of Gonda district).

The mahant of the Udaseen sect at that time was an old sadhu, Keshav Das – considered the most worthy disciple of Narayan Das, the man largely credited with making the order a pan-India phenomenon. Narayan Das died in 1923 and the mantle of authority passed on to Keshav Das. In the late 1940s, Mahant Keshav Das began taking opium and soon became an addict. As the drug was not available readily, he was always on the lookout for it.

Partly due to this lack of regular supply of the drug, Keshav Das walked into a trap laid for him by K.K.K. Nair. The mahant's addiction was an opportunity Nair exploited to rob the Udaseen sect of its possessions in Ayodhya and nearby areas. In the span of a few months in late 1949 and early 1950, Nair established complete control over the mind and body of Keshav Das. Dangling opium in front of him, he left the mahant in such a state that he transferred most of the landholdings of the Ranopali Nanakshahi Temple to Nair's family members. According to Sadhu Saran Mishra, a Faizabad-based advocate whom Nair hired as his attorney after the case entered the district civil court,

> Mahant Keshav Das was more a scholar than a sadhu. He led a quiet and simple life. But in his old age, he began taking opium and soon turned into an addict. This proved fatal for him as well as for Ranopali Ashram. Apart from this addiction, Keshav Das had no other weakness. He was not a worldly man and did not realize what he was doing. When Nair got to know about his addiction, he started inviting him frequently and supplying him with opium, and in 1949–50 he got him to transfer the ownership of most of the ashram's land to his family members.[2]

This silent expropriation of the temple land did not remain a secret for long. Soon, some of the Udaseen sadhus got to know about the development, and discontentment started brewing against Keshav Das. Baba Damodar Das, Keshav Das's secretary, took the lead in this rebellion. On 3 December 1951, Keshav Das was forced to leave the abbotship, and Baba Ramgopal Das was made the new mahant of the sect. This is what Sadhu Saran Mishra said about the turn of events:

> In 1953, a civil suit was filed in the court of the civil judge, Faizabad, on behalf of Baba Ramgopal Das. The suit claimed that Keshav Das had transferred all the pattas, not out of his free will, but under pressure and as such they were not legal. The case passed through several ups and downs. First it was won by the ashram, and Nair accepted the Ranopali Temple's right over the land but later he revived his claim and finally won the case in 1976.[3]

By this time, however, the land ceiling law was in place, and it rendered Nair's victory meaningless. His landholdings as well as those of his family members had already crossed the statutory ceiling. It was obvious that the moment this judgment was made effective, the entire land belonging to the Ranopali Temple would be taken over by the government under the ceiling law. There was, therefore, hardly anything in this victory for Nair to rejoice in. On the advice of Sadhu Saran Mishra, he decided to return the land to the Udaseen sect if the latter paid him the expenditure that he had incurred on the case. The issue was thus resolved, and the land grabbed by Nair was restored to the Udaseens.

For Nair, opium was just one of the means. What helped him even more in his quest for land was the nexus that had converted the Babri Masjid into a temple, in particular, his friendship with Mahasabha leaders like Mahant Digvijai Nath and Gopal Singh Visharad, as well as with powerful vairagis in Ayodhya. Many senior residents of Ayodhya however argue that the role this group played in providing Nair with huge tracts of land was primarily because this was seen by the Mahasabhaites and vairagis as a way to return the favour done to them by the former district magistrate of Faizabad.

Close on the heels of the 'miracle' in the Babri Masjid, real estate gifts started pouring in for Nair. Among the most notable was a massive mango orchard, euphemistically called Lakhperwa Bagh. The name was derived from the fact that it had one lakh trees. A prominent Ramanandi establishment is said to have played a key role in the transfer of this orchard on the Faizabad–Rae Bareli road in the name of Nair.

Equally significant in this context was the role of Mahant Digvijai Nath – whose friendship with zamindars and petty kings in the region was pretty well known – in adding to the land acquisition efforts of Nair.[4] Nair was not the sole beneficiary of these efforts. Some of his close associates too benefited from them, one such being Gopal Singh Visharad. An indication of how Visharad gained from his proximity to Nair and the kind of role Mahant Digvijai Nath played in this land acquisition drive is clear from a letter that Visharad wrote to the mahant on 2 July 1951:

> Your recent visit brought about a spring in the hearts of Hindus, which alone is our sole inspiration to work for a Hindu Rashtra [...] Recently I met Nair Saheb. He has asked me to convey to you a message that you please tell the landholder of Khiri Lakhimpur, with whom both you and Nair have already discussed the land deal, to meet Nair Saheb as early as he can.
>
> Nair Saheb has also promised to give me 200 bigha from that holding, saying that I don't have enough land-base. I have never expressed such a wish to him; he is doing this on his own. Such people are very few in this world.[5]

Nair's tenure in Faizabad was the most uncertain period for zamindars and small-time rajas. In 1949–50, when Nair was busy in self-aggrandisement, the fiefdoms of the zamindars and petty kings – the by-products of the British Raj – had begun to collapse. The Zamindari Abolition and Land Reforms Bill was introduced in the UP Assembly in July 1949 and passed on 16 January 1951, but could become operational only after the Supreme Court upheld the Act on 5 May 1952.

It was also the period when these landlords were being crushed under the pressure of accumulated taxes which were due to the province. This situation led the government to bring, just before the abolition of the zamindari system, an Encumbered Estates Act, which empowered the government to acquire the properties of defaulters. Advocate Sadhu Saran Mishra, the man who looked after Nair's civil cases in Faizabad, recounted:

> Nair sensed an opportunity for himself in this. In lieu of clearing government dues, he began acquiring huge plots held by different estates in the region. One of the biggest properties he acquired thus belonged originally to the Lorpur Estate. Called Lorpur House, it was situated in the midst of a sprawling campus in the Civil Lines area of Faizabad. For some time it remained Nair's residence and was later sold off as small residential plots, giving rise to what is now known as 'Nair Colony' in the heart of the city.[6]

Similar cases were reported from Santhari village, Tikri in Gonda District and in the Palia Shahbadi area close to Civil Lines in Faizabad. On many occasions, Nair grabbed massive plots simply by misusing his official position. Whatever be the extent of such misuse of power, by the end of Nair's tenure in Faizabad, from God to ordinary mortals, all became his victims.

II

The man who understood K.K.K. Nair the best, Akshay Brahmachari, was also the one who first comprehended the ominous design behind the Ayodhya strategy of the Hindu Mahasabha. Brahmachari, like a true Gandhian, was a compassionate and an uncompromising secularist and a high-spirited politician who believed in non-violence. He was tall and heavy-set, and dressed with careless elegance in hand-spun coarse white lungi and kurta. He kept his face and head clean-shaven and used to apply three vertical lines of chandan, called tripunda, on his forehead. He had an effeminate voice and there was an intense look in his eyes.

In 1949, this thirty-three-year-old, who at that time was the secretary of Faizabad District Congress Committee and a member of the Provincial Congress Committee of UP, was much distressed at the way Hindu communalists were inching towards the Babri Masjid. As early as in the middle of November 1949, when the communalists were busy digging up Muslim graves and desecrating the graveyard outside the mosque, Brahmachari personally visited the spot and raised the issue with District Collector K.K.K. Nair, unaware that everything was happening with the connivance of the administration. It did not take him long to realize the truth. For, barely hours after he discussed the issue with Nair, a group of communalists barged into Brahmachari's house and assaulted him brutally. This happened on 15 November 1949[7] – over a month before the mosque was surreptitiously grabbed.

Brahmachari continued to protest against the communal campaign carried out by Mahasabhaites and *Virakta*, before the idol was actually placed inside the mosque. He did not spare even Congress leaders, including Baba Raghav Das, for their role in creating the atmosphere in which it became impossible for the Muslims of Ayodhya to come out and legally defend their claim to the Babri Masjid.

Moreover, when the mosque was overtaken by the band of intruders led by Abhiram Das, it was Brahmachari who first reminded Nair of his duty to remove the idol and restore the Babri Masjid to its original possessors. In his memorandum to the then home minister of UP, Lal Bahadur Shastri, on 20 February 1950, Brahmachari said the idol could have easily been removed even on 23 December 1949 had Nair wanted the idol removed:

> I went to the Babri Mosque with the District Magistrate at about 12 noon (on 23 December 1949). The image was kept there. Some people had gathered near the mosque. At that moment the mosque could have been easily saved and the image removed, but the District Magistrate did not think it proper.[8]

Nair was obviously not interested in resolving the issue, but Brahmachari was not one to give up his fight. He persisted with his protest even if it meant travelling all alone, for all those who mattered in Ayodhya and Faizabad seemed to have ganged up against the mosque, and Muslims were too frightened to come out in his support. Communalists, who roamed the streets of Ayodhya without any fear, started calling him an 'Islamophile' and the 'real trouble maker', and within days, Brahmachari was forced to leave Ayodhya. Once he left, the mob broke open the lock and occupied his house.

But this only strengthened Brahmachari's resolve to fight against the crime. For he knew that what was happening in Ayodhya had nothing to do with the religious or historical beliefs of any community but was part of a larger political design, and that if the crime went unpunished, the perpetrators would be emboldened and use yet another issue to whip up communal passion.

It was this understanding that led him to see the capture of the Muslim graveyard and the Babri Masjid in conjunction with a series of other developments that occurred simultaneously in Ayodhya and Faizabad. One of them involved the arbitrary manner in which K.K.K. Nair dispossessed a nationalist Muslim of his restaurant, Star Hotel, in Faizabad. The basis for Nair's act was a fictitious allegation by a fictitious character, and the objective was simply to harass one of the leading Muslims of Faizabad so as to terrorize the community as a whole. K.G. Mashruwala – famous Gandhian and the editor of *Harijan*, a weekly founded by Mahatma Gandhi – reported in *Harijan*'s issue dated 19 August 1950:

> An informer informed the Collector one day that there were arms hidden in that hotel. A search was made but nothing of the kind was recovered. Four men were found on the premises. One of them was from Sultanpur. He had come to this hotel to purchase biscuits. He was arrested under Section 109 [of the Criminal Procedure Code]. He was released later on. The District Magistrate ordered the proprietor of the hotel to vacate it and actually got it vacated in his own presence there and then. Later, possession of the shop was given to another person, who started his own hotel in it and called it 'Gomati Hotel'. Its opening ceremony was performed by the District Judge himself, other government officials being also present. It is said that the proprietor of 'Star Hotel' is an old nationalist Muslim and at one time he had been boycotted by the Muslim League for his nationalist views ...

The incident took place days before the idol was placed in the mosque. According to Muhammad Ahmad, son of Star Hotel's proprietor Muhammad Bashir, the incident created so much insecurity among local Muslims that it almost triggered a fresh wave of migration to East Pakistan (which later became Bangladesh). Muhammad Ahmad, who was merely eight years old in 1949, has vivid memories of the time:

> Some cobblers and horse-cart owners used to live outside our house. One night after this incident, they suddenly migrated to East

> Pakistan. Some Muslims, who had stayed back, then came to my father and requested him not to leave Faizabad. They said that if he migrated, most Muslims would go. Although the shutting down of Star Hotel was a big blow, my father decided to stay back. I saw him selling biscuits in a bucket that he carried on his head. A few months later, in 1950, my father won the case. Though we did not get Star Hotel, my father felt relieved because he had proved his innocence.[9]

To force Muslims to migrate to West or East Pakistan was perhaps the aim of Nair and other Hindu communalists. For Bashir, who faced them bravely and had to start from scratch, the hard work paid off, and before his death in 1998, he opened a new bakery – one of the best known in Faizabad today and run by Bashir's grandsons under the supervision of Muhammad Ahmad – next to what was once Star Hotel.

There were several other cases of harassment of Muslims in Ayodhya and Faizabad during late 1949 and early 1950. In one particular instance, in early 1950, once again reported by Akshay Brahmachari himself, the body of a Muslim woman was not allowed to be buried by Hindu communalists, and the administration simply refused to help them. The relatives of the woman kept running for twenty-two hours from one graveyard to the other and finally had to bury the body outside the limits of Ayodhya. Brahmachari listed many other similar cases that caused trauma to the Muslims of Ayodhya during that period.

To the Gandhian who had been forced out of Ayodhya, these seemingly isolated incidents were intrinsically interlinked, and all had the same objective – the complete Hindutvization of Faizabad district. Akshay Brahmachari could see the key role Nair was playing in generating a political atmosphere conducive to the growth of Hindu communalist politics. It was easy for Nair to shield Hindu zealots who disregarded Muslim rights or to do favours for the vairagis of Ayodhya and merchants of Faizabad who were willing patrons of Hindu communalism. It was, therefore, pointless to seek help from the district administration. The state government, too, seemed utterly callous, and so was the Congress leadership in UP.

Yet Akshay Brahmachari continued to send wake-up calls to the higher-ups, believing that good sense would ultimately prevail upon those in authority, particularly in Lucknow, and attempts would be made to undo the wrongs of the night of 22 December 1949. But when even the legal course seemed to be getting hijacked with the evident misuse of Section 145 of the Criminal Procedure Code of 1898, he was left with no option but to take recourse to the path shown by the man he had followed all his life.

Fast unto death was the sole means at the disposal of Akshay Brahmachari now, and he used it without wasting any time. On 17 January 1950, a day after Gopal Singh Visharad's suit seeking permission to use the Babri Masjid as a temple and calling for an injunction against the removal of the idol from the mosque was admitted in the civil court of Faizabad, he wrote a short and straight letter to Lal Bahadur Shastri, expressing his distress at the government's reaction to the developments in Ayodhya and declaring his intention to sit on a fast unto death from 26 January 1950 to force the government to take appropriate action in the case.

> I regret that in spite of my repeated efforts, I have not been able to impress upon you the magnitude of the recent happenings in Ayodhya. I feel that after the supreme sacrifice of [the] respected Mahatma Gandhi our hearts have been filled with fear and dread, instead of remorse and determination to carry on the issues for which he died. I also feel that we are lacking the courage to draw the masses towards the ideals of the Father of the Nation. It seems that a small incident at Ayodhya is assuming great importance in the politics of the country. If we had been a little careful in the beginning, we would certainly have checked it.
>
> Today not only [are] the members of the communal organization [...] busy in spreading communal poison for their political ends, but some responsible Congressmen have also not been able to keep themselves unaffected in the prevailing atmosphere.

> It is my firm belief that to root out the poison and to establish the ideals of Mahatmaji, we should follow the path of sacrifice which he had adopted, for this is the only way which can lead us to success.
>
> Therefore, I have decided to begin a fast unto death from the morning of 26th January 1950, at the door of the P.C.C. [Provincial Congress Committee] office, Lucknow.[10]

The fast could not begin on 26 January; it was the day the nation adopted its Constitution, declaring India a secular republic. However, it began four days later, on 30 January 1950, and soon created ripples in both Lucknow and Ayodhya.

In Ayodhya, it was received as a ray of hope by the Muslims, but they were too scared to come out in open support of Akshay Brahmachari. The Mahasabha and *Virakta*, on the other hand, instantly began a campaign to deflect the attention from the issues being raised through the fast. A telegram was sent to Akshay Brahmachari appealing to him to break his fast because the 'Muslims in Ayodhya did not have any problems'.[11] In order to provide authenticity to the telegram, twenty-one Muslims of Ayodhya were forced to sign it.

Similarly, *Virakta*, the Hindi weekly edited by Mahasabha activist Ramgopal Pandey Sharad, came out with a communiqué (vigyapti), saying that 'all that was claimed by Akshay Brahmachari was a lie. There has been no Hindu–Muslim riot in Ayodhya since 1934; neither has any Muslim house been burnt nor has anyone from the community been killed. The relationship between Hindus and Muslims in Ayodhya is as good as it was earlier. As for the Babri Masjid, the issue is being considered by the court, and whatever [the] court decides will be acceptable to both the parties.'[12] As in the case of the telegram, the communiqué, too, was published under the signature of ten-odd Muslims of Ayodhya.

The provincial government of Govind Ballabh Pant could also not ignore Akshay Brahmachari's fast. Days after it began, Lal Bahadur Shastri succeeded in persuading the Gandhian to break his fast by assuring him that the government would take suitable steps to deal with the communal trouble in Ayodhya and Faizabad and that the will of the government to do so had been strengthened by his fast. Brahmachari ended his fast on 4 February 1950.

However, since the government continued to be callous, Brahmachari pursued his struggle relentlessly. A fortnight later, 20 February 1950, he wrote another letter – together with a detailed memorandum on the situation in Ayodhya and Faizabad – to Lal Bahadur Shastri:

> After having temporarily abandoned my fast, I was laid up with fever and till very recently I was lying in the Provincial Congress Committee office. As such, I could not trouble you in that connection for some time. But unfortunately I have painfully learned that the situation in Ayodhya and Faizabad has been progressively deteriorating, and provocative speeches as well as demonstrations are still [the] order of the day. Some respectable Muslims have been assaulted because they have refused to proclaim that Babri Masjid has always been a Hindu temple, as some communalist Hindus wanted [them] to do. Propaganda for the social boycott of Muslims is freely carried on. The Muslims are terrorized and they are sending away their families to relations [sic] at safer places. Some have even fled.
>
> [...] I very much regret that till the writing of this letter nothing has come to my knowledge to show that any step has been taken to improve the situation. Whatever is being done in Ayodhya in the name of religion and historical belief is only a means for the fulfilment of political ambitions of certain people through terroristic methods. If, in the face of such grave danger, we relax our efforts to fight it out, these people would bring up other knotty problems to create further troubles, so that the power of the Congress would be shattered and their fascistic ambitions fulfilled ...[13]

Brahmachari remained seriously ill for some time, but as soon as he recovered, he was back in action and began sending one reminder after another to Shastri. But a complete silence from the other side made him feel cheated, and he started thinking of a fresh satyagraha against the government. This he made clear in his letter to Shastri dated 31 May 1950. Apart from pointing out the callousness on the part of the government in dealing with 'the situation and happenings there [Ayodhya]', the letter also gave an ultimatum and said that he would restart his fast 'if no satisfactory action is taken by 15 June next'.[14]

Three days before the deadline set by Brahmachari, Shastri replied, saying that Ayodhya's situation was better now and that the government could not do much because the case was pending in the court of law.[15]

The UP government's attitude being evasive, Brahmachari knew that further correspondence would hardly yield any result. He, therefore, decided to take recourse to yet another fast unto death and expose the government in the eyes of the people. But before doing that, he sent to Shastri a long list of instances in which the government's intervention could have improved the situation in Ayodhya and Faizabad. In this letter, written on 26 June 1950, he raised, among other issues, questions about why no action was taken against those responsible for communal troubles in the last few months as also those still indulging in provocative activities through speeches, handbills, newspapers and the like, and why no compensation was paid to the victims. It also referred to the government's failure to restore various graves and mosques – other than the Babri Masjid – which had been taken over by the communalists in Ayodhya. The letter also pointed out the government's inability to hand over Star Hotel to its legal owner in spite of a judgment in the latter's favour by a court of law.

> Thus there are innumerable questions which have no bearing on or relation with the problem of Babri Masjid and which, if properly solved, would have certainly eased and improved the situation. But, on the contrary, even today members of the minority community are subjected to various kinds of harassment and injustice. The miscreants, as I have mentioned in my memorandum, have got emboldened by their successes and they are busy creating a situation wherein the very existence of Muslims would become impossible.

> [...] You will excuse me for saying that the government has entirely failed and proved impotent in performing its duties in Faizabad and Ayodhya. Now the only way open to me is the way shown by Bapu [Mahatma Gandhi]; and, therefore, I am obliged to resume my fast. But before that I think it necessary to publish all the facts about the happenings in Ayodhya and Faizabad and the correspondence exchanged between you and me in this connection. I will wait for your reply and consent in this regard till 10 July, whereafter I will fix up a date according to my inner light and Shri Rama's inspiration and start my fast again.[16]

Simultaneously, Brahmachari took the battle to Delhi. On 8 July 1950, he had a long meeting with Nehru to whom he explained in detail all the happenings in Ayodhya and Faizabad as well as the apathetic attitude of the provincial government. The very next day, Nehru wrote to Lal Bahadur Shastri, drawing his attention towards the gravity of the situation and expressing his fear 'that we are heading again for some kind of disaster'.[17]

As directed by Nehru, Brahmachari discussed the issues with Shastri on 13 July, but nothing substantial came out. Finally, on 24 July 1950 he wrote to Shastri:

> From all your talks and correspondence it seems that the government does not want to touch upon the basic elements of the problem. I have also failed in drawing the attention of Congress leaders towards the terrible situation [prevailing] in Ayodhya. I am, therefore, obliged to resume my fast, which I had abandoned on 4 February 1950. I will restart my fast from the morning of 22 August. I must thank you in the end for your cordial attitude towards me.[18]

As promised, Akshay Brahmachari began his second fast outside the Provincial Congress Committee office in Lucknow. This was to be a marathon fast, continuing for thirty-two days. Explaining the rationale behind his second fast he said:

> I do not see the developments in Ayodhya and Faizabad merely in the context of a religious feud over temple and mosque. I rather see

> them in the light of citizen's rights. If a citizen has to live in this country and if he is a believer, then he must have a right to have a place of worship too. If he has the right to live in this country, then, after his death, he must also have the right to have a piece of land for his cremation or burial. No regime can be called democratic if it violates these basic rights of citizens. And if, on historical ground[s], a temple is converted into a mosque or a mosque is converted into a temple, then let the government accept it in principle and form a committee of historians to decide as to which temple was converted into mosque in the past. In that case, we will also have to think where the history should stop. Moreover, those who want to compromise today with the people trying to finish off Muslims should also be ready for the fact that tomorrow these very people, in order to promote their fascist politics, would behave similarly with Harijans and day after tomorrow with Sikhs and four days later the country would get fragmented into Vaishnav area, Shaiv area and many such pockets. And all this would lead to chaos and Hitler's brand of terrorism which will destroy the democracy.[19]

With these words, Brahmachari began his fast, which remained a low-key affair for quite some time. But as time progressed, ripples began to be felt in the corridors of power. On 31 August, an MLA, Fakhrul Islam, raised the issue in the Legislative Assembly during Question Hour. Replying to a volley of questions on the communal tension in Faizabad, Home Minister Lal Bahadur Shastri tried to present a picture that all was well in the district. When a member asked whether he was aware of Brahmachari's fast, Shastri first tried to feign ignorance, but when other members joined in, he had to admit that he was aware of the developments but did not commit to anything.[20]

Again, on 6 September 1950, the issue came up in the form of an adjournment motion in the Assembly. But despite a heated debate on the floor of the House, the motion could not be accepted by the chair as the government was adamantly opposed to it. The continuing fast, however, kept the heat on the members of the Legislative Assembly. The issue had now become a talking point, though the government was still not ready to talk to the Gandhian.

On 14 September 1950, the Ayodhya issue rocked the Assembly for the third time. The issue came up in the form of a question and soon the number of supplementaries started piling up. Despite Shastri trying his best to defend the government, the issue threatened to go out of hand, forcing Chief Minister Govind Ballabh Pant to intervene and read out a detailed statement on various incidents that had occurred in Ayodhya and Faizabad.[21] After his statement, there took place in the Assembly a small debate, to which Pant replied saying:

> I have said that I do not wish that there should be any obstruction to any one in the enjoyment of any right whatever. If any thing, which was improper, did take place, we tried to remedy it. We have regret for those who were put into distress on its account. We were not less worried than they for such acts. It is our object and our desire that all people should live in amity and every one should enjoy the full benefit of his rights, and the atmosphere of our state should be such that none should have any cause to feel that there is any danger to him in residing here, or that he cannot live here with honour, self-respect, joy and peace.[22]

Pant's statement ended the debate in the Assembly for the time being, but he had promised nothing and had merely glossed over the issue. Akshay Brahmachari, therefore, continued with his fast, which had already entered its fourth week. He had become very weak, and his health was deteriorating fast. It was in these circumstances that two prominent Gandhians of the time – Vinoba Bhave and K.G. Mashruwala – intervened to prevail upon Brahmachari to end his fast. Shastri, too, wrote a personal letter referring to Pant's reply in the Assembly and appealing to him to break his fast. Mashruwala, who was also a friend of the fasting Gandhian, wrote in *Harijan* that Brahmachari still felt hesitation in accepting these assurances as sufficient and that his apprehensions were not quite groundless.[23]

Although Akshay Brahmachari broke his fast on 22 September 1950 under pressure from his friends and well-wishers, the struggle of this lone warrior continued. He spent the rest of his life attempting to resolve the Babri Masjid–Ramajanmabhoomi problem and to deepen the roots of communal harmony. But it was a silent struggle all through. And when he died after a prolonged illness in Mayo Hospital in Lucknow on 28 April 2010, only a small group of his friends and his long-term companion Meera Behn felt the loss. The Akshay Brahmachari Ashram in Chinhat on the outskirts of Lucknow still carries on the mission the Gandhi of Ayodhya had set for it.

III

The Hindu Mahasabha succeeded in capturing the Babri Masjid. But it still had to take the Ayodhya strategy to its logical end and could hardly expect it to create waves on its own. So far, the party had been successful in using to its advantage the changed configuration in Ayodhya – and in UP – after Partition and the conspiracy that succeeded in placing the idol in the mosque. But, as the unfolding events revealed, the Mahasabha could not take it further to trigger a large-scale mobilization of Hindus. The Mahasabha could not sustain for long the communalist propaganda that it started immediately after taking over the mosque, and the gains the party had made in the first few months after 22 December 1949 started vanishing.

One of the reasons for the Mahasabha's inability to do so was that, once the Constitution was adopted on 26 January 1950, secularism became one of the pillars of independent India. As the trauma started healing, the mood of the nation started changing.

This was due, in large part, to Jawaharlal Nehru whom the post-Partition frenzy had put at odds with Hindu communalists, belonging to the Mahasabha and the RSS, as well as with Hindu traditionalists inside his own party who seemed almost ready to join hands with zealots outside the Congress to launch mobilization campaigns on communal lines. In fact, it was the threat of this new inter-party equation – between Hindu traditionalists within the Congress who accepted the primacy of Hindu values and the Mahasabhaites and other communalists who championed the cause of a Hindu Rashtra – that appeared more ominous to Nehru than the threat posed by the Hindu communalists per se.[24] Understandably, therefore, Nehru's fight against Hindu communalism had to remain first and foremost his struggle to marginalize Hindu traditionalists within the Congress.

It took Nehru almost a year after the adoption of the Constitution – as well as the Mahasabha's onslaught on the Babri Masjid – to make secularism emerge as the norm of the Indian political system and to effectively marginalize Hindu traditionalists inside the Congress and thus, by choking this source of strength, to weaken the organizations identified with Hindu communalism beyond redemption. In the process, the troubles being fomented at the grass-roots level could not find enough scope – or conducive ground – to get magnified enough to be exploited politically.

Indeed, the Mahasabha had badly misjudged Nehru's ability to outmanoeuvre communalists. The post-Partition context had given the Mahasabhaites hope that they could exploit the situation arising from the trauma of Partition – a hope that was quashed in the aftermath of Mahatma Gandhi's assassination. But later, their successful collaboration with Congress traditionalists in Ayodhya revived this hope.

To Nehru's further dismay, this partnership was not just restricted to Ayodhya and UP, but had started showing up on higher planes as well. Many Congress members seemed to agree with the views of Syama Prasad Mookerjee, arguably the most articulate voice of Hindu communalists in the Parliament, and Purushottamdas Tandon, the Congress heavyweight in UP who symbolized the communal outlook of a section of the party. Such was the influence of closet communalism on a section of the Congress party that the *Times of India* commented in its edition on 17 August 1950:

> Congressmen belonging to this school of thought want to see the end of the policy of appeasement of Pakistan by Congress, which, they say, has continued even after [the] partition of the country. They seem to support Dr Mookerjee and Mr Purushottamdas Tandon in their approach of these problems. They feel that it is not a question of supporting communalism or opposing secularism as the Prime Minister would like to interpret it, but one of showing grit and strength towards Pakistan, who, they say, is determined to be anti-Hindu in her policies and aggressive towards India as a whole.[25]

These developments were significant from the point of view of the way they were contributing to intra-party power struggles in the Congress which had started once the idealism of the freedom struggle ceased to remain a viable constraint on political venality and with Mahatma Gandhi no longer around to broker peace. In particular, the Congress members in favour of employing closet communalism for political ends were strengthening the efforts by Sardar Vallabhbhai Patel and his faction of Hindu conservatives to neutralize Nehru. This struggle within the party sometimes even led the conservative section of the Congress leadership to use communalism as a tool.

While Patel had taken vigorous action against the RSS and the Hindu Mahasabha following the assassination of Mahatma Gandhi, he did not hesitate to press for some recognition of Hinduism in India's national life.[26] In fact, one of the arguments used in Mahasabha circles against the resumption of political activity in 1949 was that it was not necessary since Sardar Patel was pursuing a strong Hindu policy.[27]

Many argue that in the years after Independence, neither Nehru nor Patel trusted each other's intentions. Even as the two leaders avoided any confrontations in the party, Nehru was forced to opt for cautious moves, which were borne out of his understanding that a premature showdown with Hindu conservatives in the party might not be to his advantage. This may have been the reason why Nehru, despite expressing his distress, and later helplessness, regarding the developments in Ayodhya, did not exhibit a confrontationist attitude towards the premier of the United Provinces, Govind Ballabh Pant, who was a staunch loyalist of Patel.

Around the time when Pant was showing defiance, despite the fact that Nehru had repeatedly expressed concern about the developments in Ayodhya, in Delhi, the intra-party fight started showing signs of intensifying. On 2 May 1950, Nehru shared his anguish with his chief ministers:

> It is extraordinary how soon some of us have forgotten one of the basic principles and planks of the Congress – inter-communal unity [...] We have talked about a secular state. Often enough, those who have talked about it have understood it least and belied it by their own words and action.[28]

It is believed that in making these observations, Nehru probably had in his mind the situation in UP, where communal tendencies had been quite pronounced at that time.[29] But his distress was also partly due to the way Patel was pushing the name of Purushottamdas Tandon for the post of party president.

Purushottamdas Tandon was the person chiefly responsible for creating an atmosphere in UP which made closet communalism a credible tactic. He was highly articulate and had a magnetic political personality. The secret of his popularity was as much due to his powerful rapport with the masses through his long association with the agrarian movements of the 1920s and '30s as his fanatic dedication to the causes dearest to conservative Congress members and communalists – Hindi, Hindus and Hinduism. He was the man who, perhaps more than any other, personified the Hindu traditionalist current of opinion in the party after 1947. From 1948 onwards, Tandon, as president of the Congress unit in UP, spoke out increasingly against Indian Muslims preserving their own specific identity, as in June that year in Sultanpur:

> The Musulmans must stop talking about a culture and a civilization foreign to our country and genius. They should accept Indian culture. One culture and one language will pave the way for real unity. Urdu symbolizes a foreign culture. Hindi alone can be the unifying factor for the diverse forces in the country.[30]

Nehru did nothing to hide his consternation about his own inability to restrain the political momentum that Tandon had gained weeks before the elections for the presidency of the party. On 8 August 1950, he wrote a letter to Tandon, trying to dissuade him from contesting the elections. Nehru justified his advice by pointing out:

> Unfortunately, you have become, to a large numbers of people in India, some kind of a symbol of this communal and revivalist outlook and the question rises in my mind: Is the Congress going that way also? If so, where do I come into the picture, whether it is the Congress or whether it is the Government run by the Congress? Thus the larger question becomes related to my own activities.[31]

As Tandon remained unrelenting, Nehru made a last-ditch effort on the eve of the elections when he explained to Patel – in his letter that was dispatched on 28 August 1950 – that because of his 'communal and revivalist outlook', Tandon was 'widely supported' by the Mahasabha and the RSS. Nehru laid down the reasons why Tandon's presidency of the Congress would not be good for the party:

> At no point during these two months and much earlier did I have any doubt in my mind that Tandon's election would be bad for the Congress and the country and should be opposed. Whenever any occasion arose for it, I made this clear. Further, I made it clear that in the particular context of events today his election would affect my position greatly and make it difficult for me to continue in the Working Committee and as Prime Minister. It was with the specific purpose of making this clear that an informal meeting of the

> Working Committee was called. I spoke to them quite frankly and left no doubt in anyone's mind there.
>
> [...] My decision was that I could not serve in the Working Committee if Tandon was president. That held whatever the Congress might decide. That decision was taken for two major reasons: that Tandon had pursued during the past two years and was still pursuing a policy which, to my thinking, was utterly wrong and harmful and his election would undoubtedly give an impetus to this policy, and I must dissociate myself completely from it. Secondly, because the election was becoming more and more a [clash] between varying policies and Tandon became a kind of symbol of one [of these policies], and was as such being supported widely by Hindu Mahasabha and RSS elements.[32]

All through, Sardar Patel consistently backed his protégé. Despite Nehru's reservations, he did not believe Tandon to be in disagreement with the ideals of the Congress. Indeed, Patel had his own calculations. His recognition of positive qualities in the proponents of Hindu Rashtra seems to have been based on his hope, rather anticipation, that their incorporation in the Congress would soften their extremist tendencies and, once their ideology became diluted, remove a current of militant opposition which could then be a source of strength for his own faction within the Congress.[33] Patel, therefore, wrote back to Nehru on 29 August 1950, asking him to shed his inhibitions with regard to 'men who have been loyal and devoted' to him all these years:

> Please suspend your judgment on the organization and the men who have been loyal and devoted to you all these years through thick and thin and test them on principles and not on personalities. Why attach so much importance to a symbol when what matters is the real thing – those principles and ideals for which the organisation stands and will stand.
>
> I plead [with] you to reflect on these words and the consequences of the contemplated action carefully and calmly and not to come to any hasty or premature convulsions.[34]

The election for the presidency of Congress were fought at the end of August 1950. For the first time in its history, the Congress had to choose between three candidates for a post which was usually uncontested. Tandon stood on a Hindu traditionalist platform with the backing of Patel, while Nehru's views were represented by two other candidates, Shankarrao Deo and Acharya J.B. Kripalani. In the event, the 3,000 delegates of the All India Congress Committee (AICC) gave Tandon a majority of 214 votes over Kripalani.

For Hindu communalists, it was indeed time to celebrate – with hesitation for some and openly for others. Thus, while the Hindu Mahasabha still kept its fingers crossed about separating Tandon from other Congress members,[35] Syama Prasad Mookerjee made no secret of his satisfaction.[36] The RSS, on its part, claimed with much self-congratulation that by choosing Tandon over Kripalani, Congress members had shown 'their preference for Gandhism plus Patelism as compared to Gandhism plus Nehruism'.[37]

For Nehru, however, it was the time of reckoning. He had achieved nothing through his protracted war against Hindu conservatives, and now the only option available to him was to declare an all-out war against the growing rapprochement between Hindu communalists and Hindu traditionalists. At the Congress session at Nasik in September 1950, just when Nehru seemed to be losing hold over the party, he came out of his shock and depression, and hit back with full force on the issue of communalist ideas penetrating a party that was founded on secular ideals:

> If injustice is done to minorities in Pakistan, is it a valid reason to adopt a similar attitude here? If that is called democracy then I say, hell with such democracy [...] True that people's passion had been aroused by events in Pakistan, but democratic principles could not be thrown to [the] winds because of that. Congressmen should never compromise [on] principles [...] I am Prime Minister today because you have chosen me. If you want me as Prime Minister, you have to follow my lead unequivocally. If you do not want me to remain, you tell me so and I shall go. I will not hesitate, I will not argue. I will

> go out and fight independently for the ideals of Congress as I have done all these years.[38]

During this session, Nehru regained the allegiance of many Congress members, and all the resolutions he proposed were passed. The overwhelming support he received was hailed as a significant victory for the secular state. The tide had started turning merely three weeks after Nehru seemed to have lost the battle inside the Congress. Tandon, the newly elected president of the party, found himself being so much on the defensive that he had to postpone the nomination of the Congress Working Committee (CWC). The *New York Times* in a lead article said: 'In effect, the decision made at Nasik was that India will continue along the Gandhi–Nehru line toward a secular welfare state, not toward an orthodox Hindu oligarchy.'[39]

That was the beginning of the end of the efforts by Hindu traditionalists and communalists to take the Congress in a different ideological direction. The death of Patel on 15 December 1950 accelerated the process further. It deprived Tandon of a vital ally and spread desolation throughout the Hindu communalist camp. But Nehru relentlessly waged a veritable war of attrition against Tandon, who was ultimately forced to resign within a year of being elected as the president of the Congress. The war thus won led Nehru to impose a style of politics based on secularism – a style that had no space for communal politics of the Hindu Mahasabha. The fate of the Ayodhya strategy too was sealed now. In every part of the country, including UP, communalist politics suffered from the way Nehru contested its legitimacy and repressed its propagandist activities.

However, until he succeeded in marginalizing Hindu traditionalists inside the Congress and their source of strength outside the party, Nehru seemed to have allowed his secularism to suffer from a certain ambiguity, doubtless due to his concern not to hand over his opponents a chance to brand him anti-Hindu and, thereby, score a deadly point over him. Pragmatists may argue that was the reason why Nehru, as he jostled with Patel for supremacy within the party, did not mind a great part of his vision of secularism falling by the wayside.

There is a counter-argument as well, which raises some pertinent questions. Was it necessary for Nehru to remain a mute spectator while Govind Ballabh Pant and Purushottamdas Tandon played the communal card to finish off their opponents in UP – especially Acharya Narendra Dev – and thus created a ground conducive for the Mahasabhaites in Ayodhya? Could it have been avoided? Would communalists still have succeeded in taking over the Babri Masjid and retaining it in the face of all the hue and cry, had Nehru opted for an uncompromisingly tough attitude towards them right from the beginning? Wouldn't a harder attitude have forced the state government to take effective steps to remove the idol from the mosque and, thereby, undo the wrong committed on the night of 22 December 1949? Could the Hindu Mahasabha have succeeded in going that far in implementing its Ayodhya strategy without Nehru's soft approach?

These questions might not have arisen – and the course of history would have been different – had Nehru not been so indifferent as he appeared while the Congress conservatives launched an annihilation campaign against Congress socialists, especially in UP. For, had that campaign been stopped at the very beginning, UP would not have fallen into the hands of Hindu conservatives, who were only a shade different from Hindu communalists.

One of the great mysteries of Indian history is the fact that Nehru was aware that Acharya Narendra Dev and his socialist group constituted a potential support for him – and an intra-organizational power base for the promotion of his own leftism that was saturated with a nationalist philosophy – in the event of a political showdown in the party. Patel and his group of conservatives, including Pant and Tandon, had always been opposed to what the socialists stood for. They had left no stone unturned in their efforts to block the socialists' attempts to gain entry to the party's decision-making bodies, and in the end, to compel their expulsion from the Congress.[40]

Strangely enough, Nehru, who had himself acted like a catalyst and who had been so jubilant at the time of the formation of this group within the Congress in 1934, did hardly enough to shield it – in critical moments – from Hindu conservatives. Nehru's cold indifference was visible at the time when, in February 1947, the conservative faction succeeded in getting a clause inserted in the Congress constitution, which barred membership in the party to anyone who belonged to any intra-party political group with a separate creed or constitution. It was a major tactical victory for the conservatives as it left the socialists with only two options – either 'de-partyize' the Congress socialist faction, and thus give up its structural form and the political strength that it gained from it, or simply quit and form a separate party outside the Congress. Personally, it was a massive gain for Patel, whose public statements around this time clearly showed that his views on socialists had not changed since 1934, and that he was still dismissive of their programmes of socio-economic change.

Such instances of Nehru's silence at a time when his opponents were scoring one point after the other over him continues to baffle many even today. Equally debatable is the amount of power Nehru actually possessed between 1947 and 1950, as well as the extent of his determination to use it to protect his potential intra-party allies.

However, the mystery behind Nehru's indifference to the Congress Left may well be hiding many secrets of modern Indian history.

IV

Yet, Nehru's greatest strength, besides his own charm, was his vision for a secular India, and eventually he did manage to create an atmosphere in which communal projects could not be employed for political gain. But that was not the only reason for the failure of the Ayodhya strategy. At the local level, too, the Mahasabha's plan started withering away as soon as the focus in Ayodhya shifted from capturing the Babri Masjid to sharing the booty.[41] And it happened around the same time when Nehru was imposing constraints on any strategy of ethno-religious mobilization in the country.

Soon after obtaining the judicial injunction against the removal of the idol from the Babri Masjid, the conspirators and the collaborators at the grass-roots level got together to form an organization with the avowed purpose of fighting a legal battle against the Muslims' claim over the mosque as well as organizing various janmabhoomi-centric festivals in Ayodhya. The organization was named 'Shri Rama Janmabhumi Sewa Samiti'. Though initially there were many prominent vairagis of Ayodhya in its governing body, it soon passed into the hands of a group of three: former city magistrate Guru Datt Singh, who after quitting his job became its general secretary; Gopal Singh Visharad, its joint secretary; and Ramchandra Das Paramhans, who occupied the post of its secretary-in-charge of campaigns. The samiti collected huge donations to carry out its avowed purposes. The control over its wealth now became the major focus for many in Ayodhya. Charges and countercharges followed.

Virakta was used extensively by one side to blame the other for pocketing this wealth. Its editor, Ramgopal Pandey Sharad, himself a known Mahasabhaite, held a grudge that he was kept out while the show was being managed by Visharad. Following a series of articles in *Virakta* about rampant corruption in the management of the growing wealth of the samiti, Visharad filed a defamation suit against the weekly's editor and publisher. The suit was later rejected.

Perhaps Ramchandra Das Paramhans too could not get the kind of position he had hoped for in the overall management of the samiti and access to its funds. And as such, he too started a parallel campaign alleging that Visharad was trying to pocket its funds.

A similar fight began over the donations and offerings that devotees were making at the chabutara as well as regarding the continuation of the akhand kirtan which had been started at the behest of K.K.K. Nair's wife, Shakuntala Nair, just outside the mosque on 23 December 1949. The way the donations and offerings at the new Ramajanmabhoomi were kept and used for the management of the puja engendered equal mistrust. Babu Priyadatta Ram, as the receiver for the attached property, was in charge of this wealth, but the accounts were not maintained properly and there were allegations of pilferage on a large scale. Potentially, too, the communalists' latest possession seemed highly lucrative. Issues such as future control over the whole or a part of this site also began fuelling the battle on the ground.

Avarice killed the unity among the various groups of communalists which were supposed to be the bedrock upon which the Hindu Mahasabha would have propelled its Ayodhya strategy. The general impression this created among ordinary Hindus was one of complete chaos, of a campaign that had succeeded in producing a 'miracle', but was unable to maintain its basic propriety thanks to sheer greed.

The Ayodhya strategy was dead; the fight for Ayodhya's booty now began.

Afterword

THE AYODHYA STRATEGY DID not bear fruit for Hindu communalists immediately, but the night of 22–23 December 1949 set in motion a chain of events which were to give rise to one of the most contentious issues in independent India.

The turmoil created by the planting of the idol of Rama in the Babri Masjid gave way to legal battles, and the issue remained politically dormant for over a quarter of a century. Gopal Singh Visharad's title suit was followed closely by that of Ramchandra Das Paramhans, in January 1950. In 1959, the Nirmohi Akhara joined the legal battle with its own claim over the site, and in 1961 the Sunni Central Waqf Board filed a counter title suit.

The situation, however, started changing once the Vishwa Hindu Parishad (VHP), an offshoot of the RSS, began a campaign to build a Rama Temple in Ayodhya in 1984. The Babri Masjid–Ramajanmabhoomi dispute took centre stage in February 1986 when the district court of Faizabad ordered the unlocking of the mosque and allowing the worship of the idol by devotees. In 1989, as the issue started becoming increasingly contentious, all the title suits were consolidated and transferred to the Allahabad High Court so that they could be taken up together.

The same year, in October and November, responding to the call of the VHP, kar sevaks started converging in Ayodhya, collecting pujan shila from different parts of the country for the construction of a temple dedicated to Rama. On 9 November 1989, the shilanyas of the proposed temple was performed outside the disputed area.

The rath yatra of LK Advani – one of the leaders of Bharatiya Janata Party (BJP), the political arm of the RSS – aimed at arousing Hindu sentiments in support of a Rama temple in Ayodhya in September–October 1990 further worsened the situation. In October 1992, the VHP announced the resumption of kar seva on 6 December 1992. The frenzy of the mob that converged on the Babri Masjid on that day saw the mosque being attacked and demolished.

The incident led to the issue becoming one of the most prominent factors defining the politics of the nation. The BJP, gaining strength after making this issue the central point of its politics, reaped dividends in 1998 when it formed – along with some smaller parties clubbed together as the National Democratic Alliance – the government at the Centre and remained in power for over six years.

The VHP now set a fresh deadline of 15 March 2002 to begin the construction of a temple for Lord Rama. Once again, kar sevaks from all over the country started converging in Ayodhya. It was while returning from one such trip by a group of kar sevaks that a coach of the Sabarmati Express was burnt down at Godhra, in Gujarat, followed by one of the worst pogroms India has ever seen after Independence.

Meanwhile, a three-judge bench of the Allahabad High Court began hearings on the title suits to determine the ownership of the disputed area. On 30 September 2010, the court delivered a bizarre judgment, directing the division of the disputed site among Hindus, Muslims and the Nirmohi Akhara.

However, that has not meant the end of the issue and the structure is still under dispute. The bomb is still ticking, and all eyes are fixed on the Supreme Court of India.

Cast of Characters

All India Hindu Mahasabha

Abhiram Das

A naga vairagi or militant ascetic of Ayodhya, he led a small band of Hindu fanatics and surreptitiously planted the idol of Lord Rama in the Babri Masjid on the night of 22–23 December 1949. An enthusiastic member of the Hindu Mahasabha, he was a trusted lieutenant of Mahant Digvijai Nath, the president of the UP unit of the Mahasabha. In the FIR that was lodged on the morning of 23 December 1949, he was named as the prime accused. Because of this act, he was often called Janmabhoomi Uddharak or simply Uddharak Baba. He died in 1981.

Bishan Chandra Seth

He was the general secretary of the Hindu Mahasabha's UP unit in 1949 and a confidant of Mahant Digvijai Nath.

Digvijai Nath

He was the mahant or abbot of the Gorakshapeeth in Gorakhpur in eastern UP. Till the planting of the idol in the Babri Masjid by Hindu communalists, he was the president of the Hindu Mahasabha in UP. A day later, on 24 December 1949, he was made the all-India general secretary of the party. He was one of the main accused in the Mahatma Gandhi murder case and the prime mover in the illegal occupation of the Babri Masjid.

Gopal Singh Visharad

In 1949, he was general secretary of the Faizabad unit of the All India Hindu Mahasabha (AIHM) and joint secretary of the All India Ramayan Mahasabha, the front organization of the AIHM which organized a series of events leading to the forcible occupation of the Babri Masjid in the dark hours of 22–23 December 1949. It was he who filed a petition in the civil court of Faizabad and obtained an injunction restraining the government from removing the idol of Lord Rama from the mosque.

N.B. Khare

A Hindu Mahasabha leader, he became the all-India president of the party during its twenty-eighth session, held in Calcutta during 24–26 December 1949 – the first one to be held after the assassination of Mahatma Gandhi. However, with V.G. Deshpande as national vice-president of the Mahasabha, he remained, for all practical purposes, a figurehead of the party. Earlier, he was the prime minister of the princely state of Alwar.

Ramchandra Das Paramhans

He was a naga vairagi belonging to the Digambari Akhara, one of the three main militant ascetic orders of the Vaishnava sect, and the president of the Ayodhya unit of the Hindu Mahasabha. He was also the general secretary of the All India Ramayan Mahasabha. He was supposed to accompany Abhiram Das to the Babri Masjid on the night of 22 December 1949 but vanished from Ayodhya on the eve of the event. Much later, in 1991, he claimed in an interview to the *New York Times* that it was he who placed the idol of Lord Rama in the mosque. At the time of his death in 2003, he was the mahant or abbot of the Digambari Akhara.

Ramgopal Pandey Sharad

A member of the Hindu Mahasabha in Ayodhya, he was the editor of the right-wing Hindi weekly, *Virakta*, which not only covered the 'miracle' of Lord Rama's appearance in the Babri Masjid but also took active part in it. Later, he wrote a book, *Ramajanmabhoomi Ka Rakta Ranjit Itihaas* (The Blood-soaked History of the Birthplace of Rama), which sought to bury the truth forever and immortalize the myth of the 'miracle'.

Shakuntala Nair

Wife of K.K.K. Nair, she was associated with the activities of the Hindu Mahasabha even when her husband was the deputy commissioner-cum-district magistrate of Faizabad. It was at her behest that on 23 December 1949, the very first morning after the idol of Rama was placed in the Babri Masjid, an akhand kirtan was begun near the gate of the mosque. In the very first general elections in 1952, she got elected to the Lok Sabha on a Hindu Mahasabha ticket from Gonda.

Syama Prasad Mookerjee

A senior Hindu Mahasabha leader, he was a cabinet minister in the Nehru government in the late 1940s. About a year after the assassination of Mahatma Gandhi, he quit the Mahasabha as he developed serious differences with other leaders of the party. Later, he formed the Jana Sangh, another Hindu political party which was the precursor of the Bharatiya Janata Party.

Tej Narain

The right-hand man of Mahant Digvijai Nath, he was the working president of the UP unit of the Hindu Mahasabha. It was under him that the Mahasabha started a propaganda unit – whose sole object was to use the Babri Masjid issue to mobilize Hindus on as large a scale as possible – in Ayodhya soon after the idol was planted.

V.D. Savarkar

The supreme leader of All India Hindu Mahasabha, he remained behind bars for more than a year as he was suspected of masterminding the conspiracy to assassinate Gandhi. Though eventually exonerated for lack of evidence to corroborate the testimony of the approver, he was held guilty much later during the mid-1960s when the government set up a high-level inquiry commission to investigate the conspiracy behind the assassination.

V.G. Deshpande

As national vice-president of the All India Hindu Mahasabha – a post he assumed at the Calcutta session of the party – he got involved in the task of turning the planting of the idol of Rama in the Babri Masjid into a nationwide political issue. He travelled to Ayodhya in January 1950 and got his party to observe 'Rama Janmabhoomi Day' across north India on Rama Navami (that fell on 27 March that year). Together with V.D. Savarkar and Mahant Digvijai Nath, he spent almost a year in jail following the assassination of Mahatma Gandhi.

Vishwanath Agrawal

He was in charge of propaganda in the Hindu Mahasabha's UP unit in 1949–50. He, along with Tej Narain, assisted V.G. Deshpande and Mahant Digvijai Nath in drawing a detailed political action plan for the party to mobilize Hindus immediately after the idol of Rama was placed in the Babri Masjid.

Indian National Congress

Acharya Narendra Dev

He was one of the top leaders of the Congress Socialist Party (CSP) which was formed in 1934 as a subgroup of the Indian National Congress until it broke away from the parent organization in 1948. In the by-elections to the UP Assemby the same year, the Faizabad constituency (the one he used to contest from) became a matter of prestige for the then chief minister of UP, Govind Ballabh Pant. Pant's campaign – which sought to arouse the religious sensibilities of the Hindu voters in Ayodhya – not only led to Acharya Narendra

Dev's defeat but emboldened the Hindu Mahasabha leaders in the region as well.

Akshay Brahmachari

A Gandhian, he was the secretary of the Faizabad District Congress Committee in 1949. He saw through the plans of the Mahasabha and sought to prevent the communal flare-up that the party was engineering by informing the district authorities about his suspicions, He single-handedly opposed the mobilization of vairagis and Hindu fanatics at the Babri Masjid before the idol was placed in it, and till his death in 2010, he fought relentlessly through Gandhian means for the the idol to be removed from the Babri Masjid.

Baba Raghav Das

A Gandhian based in Deoria in eastern UP, he was looked upon in the region as a saintly politician for his dedication to Hinduism. Born as Raghavendra Sheshappa Pachapurkar to a Brahmin family in Poona (Maharashtra) in 1896, he shifted to Deoria after his entire family was wiped out in a cholera epidemic. He joined the Congress party in 1920. After Independence, he was deployed by the UP chief minister, Govind Ballabh Pant, to defeat Acharya Narendra Dev in the Faizabad by-election of 1948 by arousing the communal sensibilities of the Hindus of Ayodhya.

Govind Ballabh Pant

In 1949, he was the chief minister – called premier till the Constutution was adopted on 26 January 1950 – of UP. In the state unit of the party, he led a group of conservative Congress members whose political vision contained strong Hindu revivalist overtones. He was considered close to Sardar Vallabhbhai Patel.

Jawaharlal Nehru

The first prime minister of India, he had a tempestuous relationship with Sardar Vallabhbhai Patel, especially after Independence and the assassination of Mahatma Gandhi. In the Congress, he led the secular strand of the party.

K.M. Munshi

He was the Union minister of supply in the Nehru government. A Congress leader from Gujarat, he was known for his strong Hindu sentiments. He had even left the Congress in 1941 and shifted close to the Hindu Mahasabha. He rejoined the Congress in 1946 and soon became a close confidant of Patel. After Independence, he supervised the reconstruction of the Somnath Temple at the behest of Patel.

Lal Bahadur Shastri

A Congress leader, he was the home minister of UP during the late 1940s in the provincial government headed by Govind Ballabh Pant. Later, he shifted to New Delhi, and for a period of nearly two years after the death of Jawaharlal Nehru, he was the prime minister of the country till his sudden demise.

Purushottamdas Tandon

He was the man who, perhaps more than any other, personified the Hindu traditionalist current of opinion in the Congress after 1947. Considered close to Sardar Vallabhbhai Patel, he was the president of the party in UP and Speaker of the Legislative Assembly in 1949 when the idol of Rama was planted in the Babri Masjid. In 1950, he became the all-India president of the Congress, defeating former party president Acharya J.B. Kripalani, who had the backing of Nehru.

Rafi Ahmed Kidwai

A Congress heavyweight, he led at the time of Independence the faction that was the most pragmatic and secular in the UP wing of the Congress party. He, however, fell victim to the communal smear campaign launched by the Hindu traditionalist sections of the Congress in the aftermath of Partition.

Sardar Vallabhbhai Patel

He was the powerful home minister and deputy prime minister in the Nehru government, around whom gathered the Hindu traditionalists within the Congress. His death on 15 December 1950 weakened the Hindu traditionalists in the party.

Ascetics of Ayodhya

Baba Abhay Ram Das

He is the legendary hero of the Nirvani Akhara who led the band of militant Vaishnava ascetics to Ayodhya in the eighteenth century. It is believed that it was under his leadership that the nagas of the Nirvani Akhara defeated Shaiva militant ascetics and captured the Hanuman Tilla, which later developed into Hanumangarhi. He is regarded as the first gaddi-nashin (occupant of the seat of power) of Hanumangarhi.

Balram Das

A naga vairagi, he was in 1949 the mahant or abbot of Jambwant Quila – a sprawling temple complex located close to Hanumangarhi. It was he who organized in his temple on 21 December 1949 a meeting of those who executed the Hindu Mahasabha's Ayodhya strategy on the night of 22–23 December.

Bhaskar Das

A vairagi belonging to the Nirmohi Akhara, he was a junior priest deputed in a small temple at the Ramachabutara. He later became mahant of the Nirmohi Akhara.

Dharam Das

The youngest disciple of Abhiram Das, he inherited from his guru the latter's asan or the resting place of an ascetic at Hanumangarhi, the baithak of the Nirvani Akhara. Like his guru, he is also an akharamal vairagi, and like him, he too was feared in Hanumangarhi.

Jamuna Das

In the naga lineage of Hanumangarhi, he was regarded as the religious preceptor of Abhiram Das even as the latter used to stay at the asan of another naga vairagi, Saryu Das. For, it was Jamuna Das who formally initiated Abhiram Das into asceticism and gave him the mantra, the sacred formula.

Keshav Das
He was the mahant of the Udaseen sect between 1923 and 1951. His addiction to opium led him into the trap laid by K.K.K. Nair, who, taking advantage of the mahant's condition, expropriated a good portion of the sect's landed possessions in Ayodhya and nearby areas. In 1951, when members of the sect got to know about the development, he was ousted from his post and the new mahant initiated a case against K.K.K. Nair.

Saryu Das
He was the naga vairagi who persuaded Abhiram Das to give up worldly life and become an ascetic. But as he himself belonged to a lower caste, he got Jamuna Das to initiate Abhiram Das formally. Yet, Abhiram Das stayed at Saryu Das's asan, which he inherited after the latter's death.

Satyendra Das
One of the disciples of Abhiram Das, he is presently the chief priest of the Ramajanmabhoomi Temple, a place of worship that emerged out of the surreptitious act of his religious preceptor which was carried out in the night of 22–23 December 1949.

Sitaram Das
A naga vairagi, he was, in 1949, the gaddi-nashin of Hanumangarhi.

Swami Karpatri
He was a politically ambitious sanyasi known for his knowledge of Sanskrit texts and his oratorical skills. In 1948 he founded a political party – Ram Rajya Parishad – that worked in tandem with the Hindu Mahasabha. He was a close friend of Mahant Digvijai Nath and well acquainted with most senior vairagis of Ayodhya.

Vrindavan Das
A Ramanandi vairagi belonging to the Nirvani Akhara, he assisted Abhiram Das in planting the idol of Lord Rama in the Babri Masjid. He lived in a thatched hut near the gate of the sixteenth-century mosque.

Government Officials

Abul Barkat

He was the guard positioned at the Babri Masjid on the fateful night of 22–23 December 1949. He was unaware that by the time he assumed guard at 12 o'clock of that night, Abhiram Das and his associates had already entered the mosque. Apparently, under pressure from the district administration as well as to save his job, he had to testify to being witness to the 'miracle' of the appearance of Rama's idol in the mosque that night.

Guru Datt Singh

The city magistrate of Faizabad in 1949, he was a fervent supporter of K.K.K. Nair, the deputy commissioner-cum-district magistrate of Faizabad. Like Nair, he, too, was implicated in the affair as one of the facilitators of the Hindu militants who planted the idol of Lord Rama in the Babri Masjid, and forced to retire from his post a few months after the incident.

K.K.K. Nair

Between 1 June 1949 and 14 March 1950, he was the deputy commissioner-cum-district magistrate of Faizabad. For his role in abetting the installation of the idol of Rama in the Babri Masjid, he was first asked to go on leave and then to seek voluntary retirement. He was a friend and disciple of Mahant Digvijai Nath. Later, he won the Lok Sabha elections from Bahraich on the ticket of Jana Sangh, an offshoot of the Hindu Mahasabha.

Priyadatta Ram

In 1949–50 he was the chairman of Faizabad-cum-Ayodhya Municipal Board. On 29 December 1949, when the government attached the Babri Masjid as a disputed property, he was appointed as its receiver. Babu Priyadatta Ram, as he was popularly called, took charge of the attached property on 5 January 1950 and submitted to K.K.K. Nair a 'scheme' of arrangements necessary for the upkeep of the worship of the idol installed in the mosque.

Abhiram Das's Brothers and Cousins

Awadh Kishore Jha

A cousin of Abhiram Das, in 1949 he used to stay with his elder brother Yugal Kishore Jha and his cousins Indushekhar Jha and Upendranath Mishra at a temple in Ayodhya. He was the first to reach the Babri Masjid on the morning of 23 December 1949. In 1952, he returned to his native village Rarhi in the Darbhanga district of Bihar without completing his education.

Indushekhar Jha

A cousin of Abhiram Das, he, too, used to stay with Awadh Kishore Jha, Upendranath Mishra and Yugal Kishore Jha in Ayodhya in 1949. On the night of 22 December 1949, he along with Yugal Kishore had followed Abhiram Das to the Babri Masjid. He later shifted to Mumbai.

Upendranath Mishra

Hailing from Rarhi Village in Bihar, he was the youngest brother of Abhiram Das. In 1949, he was staying in a temple that was under the control of Abhiram Das. At that time, he was studying in Maharaja Inter College, Ayodhya. After finishing his education, he took up a job in the UP government. In 2010, he returned to his native village.

Yugal Kishore Jha

The eldest among Abhiram Das's brothers and cousins staying in the temple that was under Abhiram Das's control, it was to him that Abhiram Das willed the temple in case something untoward happened to him on the night when the idol was to be planted at the Babri Masjid. Yugal Kishore accompanied Abhiram Das to the mosque that night.

Miscellaneous

Brahmadev Shastri

He was the owner of Ramesh Art Press located in the Shringarhaat area of Ayodhya. It was in this press that Hindu Mahasabha leader Gopal Singh Visharad got posters and pamphlets printed on the night of 22–23 December 1949. These materials – declaring the 'miracle' of Rama's appearance in the Babri Masjid and exhorting people to go for darshan – were used extensively to mobilize the Hindus the next morning. In 1958, he was found murdered and his elder brother, who took control of the press and renamed it 'Brahmadev Printing Press'.

Kedarnath Arya

A prominent Arya Samaj leader of Faizabad, he was an enthusiastic and generous sympathizer of Hindu militancy during the build-up to the planting of the idol of Lord Rama in the mosque. He also developed close relations with Mahant Digvijai Nath and donated a building – which later came to be used as the local office of the Mahasabha – in Ayodhya to the Hindu Mahasabha.

K.G. Mashruwala

A famous Gandhian, he was, during the late 1940s and early 1950s, the editor of *Harijan*, the journal founded by Mahatma Gandhi.

Muhammad Ismael

He was the last muezzin of the Babri Masjid. On the night of 22 December 1949, as Abhiram Das and his associates sneaked into the precincts of the sixteenth-century mosque, he put up a fierce resistance to stop the intruders. But he was alone, and was overpowered, beaten up and forced to flee in the dead of night. He spent the remaining years of his life working as a muezzin in a small mosque in Paharganj Ghosiana in the outskirts of Faizabad.

Pateshwari Prasad Singh

He was the maharaja of the princely state of Balrampur which was, in the late 1940s, part of the Gonda district of the UP. He was friends with Mahant Digvijai Nath and K.K.K. Nair.

Rajendra Singh

He is the son of Gopal Singh Visharad. By 2012, he had retired from his job and was living with his wife in Balrampur, UP.

Appendix I

THE RAMANANDI SECT IS one of many Vaishnava sampradayas, each of which advocates the worship of a different manifestation of Lord Vishnu. While in other Vaishnava sects, becoming a naga is at best a marginal phenomenon, it is a major one among the Ramanandis. There is no unanimity among historians with regard to the time when Ramananda, the founder of this sect, walked the earth, and the disputed dates vary from the end of the thirteenth to the end of the fourteenth or the beginning of the fifteenth century. The most probable date is the one provided by G.S. Ghurye, according to whom Ramananda was born in Prayag (Allahabad) in northern India in 1300 AD and spent much of his career as a Vaishnava sadhu in Varanasi.[1] The credit of establishing Lord Rama, the incarnation of Lord Vishnu, as the tutelary deity for his followers goes to Ramananda. And to the sub-sect inspired by him goes the honour of having the largest ascetic membership and the biggest contingent of nagas.

In this respect, the Ramanandi vairagis greatly resemble Shaivite sanyasis or ascetics whose military organization they seem to have copied. In naga parlance, sanyasi and vairagi designate different sectarian affiliations. While Shaiva nagas are called sanyasis, renunciants, Vaishnava nagas are referred to as vairagis, literally meaning 'detached' or 'dispassionate'. As very few historical sources are available on the origin and evolution of the Ramanandi military organization, it is extremely hard to decide upon its chronology. What is certain, however, is that the organization of akharas came very late in the life of the Ramanandi sect, much later than among the naga sanyasis of the Shaiva sect. For none of the seven major Shaiva akharas – collectively called Dashnami Sampradaya – was born later than 1600 AD and most came into existence around the tenth and eleventh centuries.[2] In contrast, the organization of Ramanandi akharas is known to have taken place between 1650 and 1700 AD.[3]

Just as the nagas of Dashnami akharas worship Lord Shiva and recognize Adi Shankaracharya as the originator of their sampradaya, the nagas of the Ramanandi sect worship Lord Rama and recognize Ramananda as their Adi Guru, deriving their main theological orientation from Tulsidas's *Ramcharitmanas*.

Externally, Ramanandi vairagis are distinguished from Shaivite sanyasis by their dress and sect marks. The vairagis are marked off from the sanyasis by their white garments as against the latter's saffron clothes. The tilak mark on the forehead of the vairagis is another feature that distinguishes them from sanyasis. The material that is used for making it is never the sacred ash, which is favoured by sanyasis. Its shape and design, too, are different and exclusively used by them. Its basic pattern is formed by three vertical lines as contrasted with the horizontal lines of the tilak mark of sanyasis. Among themselves, however, the various sub-sects of vairagis differ both as regards the material used for the tilak mark as well as the details of the pattern.

Contrary to the belief promoted largely by the All India Hindu Mahasabha as well as the Rashtriya Swayamsevak Sangh and its affiliates, including the Vishwa Hindu Parishad, that the militant akharas were organized to protect Hindu places of worship in the wake of the onslaught of Muslim rulers, history speaks otherwise. While the main driving force behind the organization of Dashnami akharas was to forcibly take over Buddhist, Jain and Vaishnava religious institutions, Ramanandi akharas came into existence primarily to protect vairagis from the violent attacks of Shaiva sanyasis and to free Vaishnava religious places from the occupation of Dashnamis.

There is evidence of how, for centuries, Shaiva and Vaishnava ascetics had been at loggerheads and had not only despised but even killed one another in fairly large numbers. Ghurye lists some such instances. It is said that one Bhairava Giri Gosavi, a Dashnami naga, had vowed not to partake of his daily meals without killing at least one Vaishnava vairagi. Among the Vaishnavas, Bhairava Giri had a counterpart in one Ram Das who refused to eat if he hadn't killed at least one sanyasi. With such deep-rooted animosity, it is not surprising why there were frequent bloody fights between them, especially at the time of the Kumbha Mela. Some of them are well recorded, including a violent fight in Hardwar in 1760, and a great massacre of vairagis by Shaiva sanyasis in Nasik during the Simhastha Fair in 1690.[4]

It is believed that against this backdrop, sometime in the late seventeenth century, a conference of Vaishnava ascetics was held at the Galta Valley, located towards the east of Jaipur in Rajasthan, in which one Balananda of the Ramanandi sect was entrusted with the task of organizing the naga section of vairagis to protect their holy places from Shaiva sanyasis, who were already well organized. Balananda is said to have formed three anis, an ani being the short form of the Sanskrit word anika, meaning 'army'.[5] These three anis – Nirvani, Nirmohi and Digambari – were subdivided into akharas, places where the militant ascetic members, the astradharis, of a traditional sect reside. The akharas affiliated with a particular sect have their own separate administrative system and are quite distinct from the mathas, the religious establishments where shastradharis or the scholastic monks of the same sect live. Each akhara operates as an individual corporate unit, but all the akharas in a sect are linked through a superior governing body.

While the Nirvani Ani consists of the Nirvani, Khaki and Niralambhi akharas, the Nirmohi Ani includes the Nirmohi, Mahanirvani and Santoshi akharas. The Digambari Ani has under it the Ram Digambari and Shyam Digambari akharas. Of all these, the Nirvani, Nirmohi and Digambari akharas are the main Ramanandi military camps, each having its principal centre in Ayodhya.

Appendix II

JAWAHARLAL NEHRU WAS CONVINCED right from the beginning that the assassination of Mahatma Gandhi was part of a much wider conspiracy by the votaries of 'Hindu Rashtra' who were planning nothing less than a seizure of power through a campaign of hate and violence. On 5 February 1948, six days after Gandhi's assassination, Nehru wrote to the heads of provinces:

> Investigations are proceeding. But enough has come to light already to show that this assassination was not the act of just an individual or even a small group. It is clear that behind him [Godse] lay a fairly widespread organization and [a] deliberate propaganda of hate and violence carried out for a long time [...] Even apart from Gandhiji's death by such assassination, the fact that there are people in this country who have adopted this method to gain political ends is of the gravest import. Perhaps we have been too lenient in dealing with these various elements in the country. We have suffered for that. But it is time that we gripped the problem fully and dealt with it adequately [...] It would appear that a deliberate *coup d'etat* was planned involving the killing of several persons and the promotion of general disorder to enable the particular group concerned to seize power.[1]

On the other hand, Sardar Vallabhbhai Patel, the then home minster, was of the opinion that the killing of the Mahatma was the handiwork of a small 'fanatical wing of Mahasabha directely under Savarkar' and not part of a larger plot. In a letter dated 26 February 1948, Nehru suggested to Patel that he display more vigour in suppressing the Hindu communalists.[2] The very next day, Patel wrote back to Nehru:

> I have kept myself almost in daily touch with the progress of the investigation regarding Bapu's assassination [...] I devote a large part of my evening to discussing with Sanjevi [director, Intelligence Bureau] the day's progress and giving instructions to him on any point that arise[s]. All the main accused have given long and detailed statements of their activities [...] It was a fanatical wing of the Hindu Mahasabha directly under Savarkar that [hatched] the conspiracy and saw it through. It also appears that the conspiracy was limited to some ten men, of whom all except two have been got hold of. Every bit of these statements is being carefully checked up and verified and scruitinised, and where necessary, followed up [...][3]

Yet Nehru was not at ease. So concerned was he that in almost every fortnightly letter, which he wrote to heads of provinces during the first two-and-a-half years of Independence, he highlighted the issue of the danger posed by communalists and urged continuous vigilance and action.[4]

Notes

Introduction

1 Based on interviews with Acharya Satyendra Das, one of the three main disciples of Baba Abhiram Das and the officially designated chief priest of Ramajanmabhoomi, and Dharam Das, the official successor of Abhiram Das held in Ayodhya on 5 November 2011.

2 Robert Lewis Gross, *The Sadhus of India*, Rawat Publications, Jaipur and New Delhi, 1992, p. 318.

3 Based on an interview with Ram Sharan Das, a ninety-two-year-old resident of Hanumangarhi, in Ayodhya on 5 November 2011.

4 See for details Justice Jeevan Lal Kapur, 'Report of the Commission of Inquiry into Conspiracy to Murder Mahatma Gandhi', New Delhi, 1970.

5 *White Paper on Ayodhya*, Government of India, February 1993, p. 1.

6 Ramgopal Pandey 'Sharad', *Shree Ramjanmabhoomi Ka Rakta Ranjit Itihaas*, Dwarika Prasad Shivgovind Pustakalaya, Ayodhya, p. 60.

7 The reconstruction of the pre-ascetic life of Abhiram Das has been based on interviews with his brother Upendranath Mishra, cousins Awadh Kishore Jha and Indushekhar Jha, and disciples Satyendra Das and Dharam Das.

8 Rajendra Prasad, *Devastated Bihar*, Bihar Central Relief Committee, Patna, 1934, p. 6

Prologue

1 The UP is the abbreviated form for the United Provinces of Agra and Oudh, popularly called the United Provinces before it was renamed as Uttar Pradesh.

Chapter 1

1 The main accused in the FIR filed on the morning of 23 December 1949 at the Ayodhya Police Station. Based on interviews with Awadh Kishore Jha and Upendranath Mishra on 21/22 November 2010 in Rarhi, Darbhanga, Bihar.

2 Awadh Kishore Jha, Abhiram Das's cousin, lived in Ramghat Temple till 1952. Thereafter, he returned to his native village, Rarhi, in the Darbhanga district of Bihar.

3 Edward A. Gargan, 'Indian Myth Sharpens Reality of Religious Strife', *New York Times*, 22 December 1991.

4 Interview with Indushekhar Jha, one of the two cousins of Abhiram Das, who had followed him into the mosque on the night of 22 Decemeber 1949. On 1 December 2010, the day he was interviewed, he was eighty-five years old and was residing in Mumbai.

5 Interview with Awadh Kishore Jha in Rarhi, Darbhanga, Bihar.

6 Based on interviews with Awadh Kishore Jha and Upendranath Mishra.

7 Van der Veer, Peter, *Gods on Earth: The Management of Religious Experiences and Identity in a North Indian Pilgrimage Centre*, Oxford University Press, Delhi, 1989, p. 146.

8 Ibid., pp. 149, 150.

9 Ibid., pp. 143, 144.

10 *Niyamavali Hanumangarhi*, Varma Printing Press, Ayodhya, 1963, pp. 1–10.

11 Gross, Robert Lewis, *The Sadhus of India*, Rawat Publications, Jaipur and New Delhi, 1992, p. 121.

12 Based on interviews with Acharya Satyendra Das and Dharam Das.

13 Based on interviews with Mahant Bhaskar Das, head of Nirmohi Akhara – who was junior priest at the Ramachabutara in 1949 – in Faizabad on 5 October 2010, and with Acharya Satyendra Das on 5 November 2010.

14 Based on interview with Awadh Kishore Jha.

15 The conversations have been reconstructed on the basis of interviews with Awadh Kishore Jha and Indushekhar Jha.

Chapter 2

1 The scene of Savarkar's Nagpur Railway Station speech has been reconstructed on the basis of the news report that appeared in the *Pioneer* on 23 December 1949, p.1. The mood of the Mahasabhaites just before their Calcutta conference – the first one to be held after the murder of Gandhi – has been recreated on the basis of interviews with people who were in at around that time.

2 The *Pioneer* (Lucknow), 23 December 1949, p. 1.

3 It has been rumoured that sometime in the second week of December 1949, at a meeting of the reception committee set up for the twenty-eighth session of the Hindu Mahasabha, Savarkar had directed Mahant Digvijai Nath, the president of the party's provincial unit in UP, to concentrate solely on 'regaining' Ramajanmabhoomi in Ayodhya so that the work could be 'accomplished' before the beginning of the Mahasabha's Calcutta session on 24 December that year. Apart from Savarkar and Mahant Digvijai Nath, it was claimed, the meeting that took place at the party headquarters in Delhi was attended by other prominent Mahasabha leaders like Nirmal Chandra Chatterjee, Dr N.B. Khare (who became the party president two weeks later) and Mamarao Date. (Based on interview with Pramod Pandit Joshi, secretary, All India Hindu Mahasabha on 10 December 2010.)

4 Hindu Mahasabha Papers, C-170, p. 12, Nehru Memorial Museum and Library (NMML).

5 N.B. Khare Papers, File No. 164, National Archives of India.

6 Christophe Jaffrelot, *The Hindu Nationalist Movement and Indian Politics: 1925 to the 1990s*, Hurst & Company, London, 1993, pp. 80–113.

7 The *Hitavada*, 3 February 1948 (p. 1), 4 February 1948 (p. 1).

8 G. Parthasarathi (ed.), *Letters to Chief Ministers*, Vol. 1, Jawaharlal Nehru Memorial Fund (JMMF), New Delhi, 1948, pp. 56–57.

9 Quoted in B. Graham, *Hindu Nationalism and Indian Politics*, Cambridge University Press, Cambridge, Massachusetts, 1990, p. 13.

10 The *Hitavada*, 17 February 1948, p. 1.

11 Ibid.

12 Ibid.

13 Hindu Mahasabha Papers, C-171 (letter from B.G. Khaparde to I. Prakash, April 1948), NMML.

14 The *Hitavada*, 10 August 1948, p. 1.

15 Justice Jeevan Lal Kapur, 'Report of the Commission of Inquiry into Conspiracy to Murder Mahatma Gandhi', Part 1, New Delhi, 1970, p. 303, para 25.106.

16 Donald Eugene Smith, *India as a Secular State*, Oxford University Press, London and Bombay, 1963, p. 474.

17 Jagdev Singh, *Ateet Tathaa Vartamaan*, Alok Prakashan, Gonda, 1975, pp. 109–13.

18 Acharya Balarao Savarkar (ed.), *Hindu Sabha Varta*, Sri Ram Janmabhoomi Visheshank, 28 October 1991, pp. 37–40. (Passage translated from the Hindi by the authors.)

19 Robert Payne, *The Life and Death of Mahatma Gandhi*, Rupa & Co., Delhi, 1997, p. 611.

20 Justice Jeevan Lal Kapur, 'Report of the Commission of Inquiry into Conspiracy to Murder Mahatma Gandhi', Part 1, p. 155, para 12B.10.

21 Ibid. p. 158, para 12B.23.

22 Durga Das (ed.), *Sardar Patel's Correspondence, 1945–1950*, Vol. 6, Navajivan Publishing House, Ahmedabad, 1973, pp. 63–64.

23 Ibid., p. 66.

24 Hindu Mahasabha Papers, F. No. 120(I), p. 7, NMML.

25 The *Statesman*, 13 June 1950, p. 7.

26 Parmanand Singh, *Legal History of the Ayodhya Litigation*, Indian Bar Review, Vol. 28 No. 2, The Bar Council of India Trust, New Delhi, 1991, p. 31.

27 *Hindustan Times*, 15 November 1947, p. 6.

28 Cited in Peter van der Veer, 'Ayodhya and Somnath: Eternal Shrines, Contested Histories', *Social Research*, 59(1), Spring 1992, p. 91.

29 Christophe Jaffrelot, *The Hindu Nationalist Movement and Indian Politics: 1925 to the 1990s*, p. 85.

30 In a controversial lecture delivered in July 1950 on 'Social Foundations of Indian Culture', K.M. Munshi said, 'We, who are blinded by an admiration of the social apparatus of the West, fail to realize that chaturvarnya [four-varna social hierarchy] was a marvellous social synthesis on a countrywide scale when the rest of the world was weltering in a tribal state.' In the same lecture, he also argued that India's 'modern renaissance' could be traced to the end of the seventeenth century when Shivaji, the Maratha king of western India, rose against the alien rule of Mughals. (K.M. Munshi, *Our Greatest Need and Other Addresses*, Bharatiya Vidya Bhawan, Bombay, 1953, pp. 43–57.)

31 V.B. Kulkarni, *K.M. Munshi*, Govt of India, New Delhi, 1983, pp. 89, 94, 100.

32 Harold A. Gould, *Grassroots Politics in India – A Centuty of Political Evolution in Faizabad District*, Oxford and IBH Publishing Co. Pvt. Ltd, New Delhi, Bombay and Calcutta, 1994, p. 161.

33 Dhananjay Keer, *Savarkar and His Times*, A.V. Keer, Bombay, 1950, pp. 3, 19–20, 25.

34 Donald Eugene Smith, *India as a Secular State*, p. 456.

35 Ibid., pp. 456, 457.

36 Harold A. Gould, *Grassroots Politics in India*, pp. 164–66.

37 Ibid., p. 179.

38 Ibid., p. 181.

39 B.R. Nanda (ed.), *Selected Works of Govind Ballabh Pant*, Vol. 12, Oxford University Press, New Delhi, 1999, p. 340. Speech at an election meeting, Faizabad, 16 June 1948, *National Herald*, 19 June 1948 (The speech was published in *National Herald* on 19 June 1948 – it is part of the *Selected Works* ...)

40 Harold A. Gould, *Grassroots Politics in India*, p. 181.

41 Jawaharlal Nehru, *Independence and After*, John Day Company, New York, 1948, p. 47.

42 Sarvepalli Gopal, *Jawaharlal Nehru: A Biography*, Vol. 2: 1947–1956, Oxford University Press, p. 92.

43 Hindu Mahasabha Papers, F. No. 120(I), p. 6 (statement of Mahant Digvijai Nath after his release from Delhi jail), NMML.

Chapter 3

1 Harold A. Gould, *Grassroots Politics in India*, p. 180.

2 Donald Eugene Smith, *India as a Secular State*, p. 474.

3 Hindu Mahasabha Papers, File No. 120(I), Resolution passed on 14 August 1949, NMML.

4 The AIRM, an Ayodhya-based organization, claimed to be an apolitical body, but it was controlled and led by three local Mahasabha leaders – Ramchandra Das Paramhans, Gopal Singh Visharad and Abhiram Das. It was under the banner of this body that the navah paath in Hanumangarhi – and later the akhand kirtan that began at the entrance of the Babri Masjid once the idol was planted – was organized. The Hindu Mahasabha as an organization carefully kept away from all these activities, but its leaders, in the capacity of AIRM leaders, took all the decisions and managed the entire show. For details see, *Aaj*, 22 December 1949, p. 5; S. Srivastava, *The Disputed Mosque: A Historical Enquiry*, Vistaar Publications, New Delhi, 1991, p. 13; Christophe Jaffrelot, *The Hindu Nationalist Movement and Indian Politics: 1925 to the 1990s*, p. 93; and Dr Radheyshyam Shukla, *Shriram Janmabhoomi*, Madhu Prakashan, Ayodhya, 1986, p. 36.

5 Dr Radheshyam Shukla, *Shriram Janmabhoomi*, p. 36.

6 Interview with Mahant Bhaskar Das. He was present at the meeting in Hanumangarhi.

7 *Aaj*, 22 December 1949, p. 5.

8 M. Chalapathi Rau, *Govind Ballabh Pant: His Life and Times*, Allied Publishers Pvt. Ltd, New Delhi, 1981, p. 366.

9 S. Gopal (ed.), *Selected Works of Jawaharlal Nehru*, Second Series, Vol. 14, Part 1, JNMF, New Delhi, 1992, p. 445.

10 Ibid., Vol. 14, Part 2, p. 296.

11 Peter van der Veer, *Gods on Earth*, p. 162.

12 Ibid., p. 162.

13 Ibid., p. 164.

14 H.R., Neville, district gazetteer of Faizabad, as mentioned in Sushil Srivastava, 'How the British Saw the Issue', in Sarvepalli Gopal (ed.), *Anatomy of a Confrontation*, Penguin Books India Pvt. Ltd, New Delhi, 1991, p. 46.

15 Sushil Srivastava, 'How the British Saw the Issue', in Sarvepalli Gopal (ed.), *Anatomy of a Confrontation*, p. 46.

16 'Papers Relating to the Dispute About the Ramchabootra', Records of the Faizabad Collectorate, as mentioned in K.N. Panikkar, 'A Historical Overview', in Sarvepalli Gopal (ed.), *Anatomy of a Confrontation*, p. 33.

17 S.K. Tripathi, 'One Hundred Years of Litigation', in Asgar Ali Engineer (ed.), *Babri Masjid-Ramjanma Bhoomi Controversy*, Delhi, 1990, pp. 218–29.

18 Harold A. Gould, 'Religion and Politics in a UP Constituency', in Donald Eugene Smith (ed.), *South Asian Politics and Religion*, Princeton University Press, Princeton, 1966, p. 62.

19 Ibid., p. 61.

20 Ibid., p. 62.

21 Peter van der Veer, *Gods on Earth*, p. 41.

22 A.G. Noorani (ed.), *The Babri Masjid Question, 1528-2003*, Vol. 1, Tulika Books, New Delhi, 2003, p. 205

23 Ibid., pp. 206, 207.

24 A.G. Noorani, 'Legal Aspects of the Issue', in Sarvepalli Gopal (ed.), *Anatomy of a Confrontation*, p. 65.

25 Rajendra Singh, son of Gopal Singh Visharad, in a personal interview on 5 November 2010 in Balrampur, UP.

26 *Aaj*, 10 December 1949, p. 2.

27 Letter from the deputy commissioner, Faizabad, dated 26 December 1949, to the chief secretary, Government of the United Provinces, in A.G. Noorani (ed.), *The Babri Masjid Question, 1528-2003*, Vol. 1, pp. 212, 213.

28 Akshay Brahmachari's 'Memorandum to Lal Bahadur Shastri, the Home Minister of UP', in A.G. Noorani (ed.), *The Babri Masjid Question, 1528-2003*, Vol. 1, p. 239.

29 Interview with Mahant Bhaskar Das. He was present at navah paath all through.

30 Akshay Brahmachari's 'Memorandum to Lal Bahadur Shastri, the Home Minister of UP', p. 239.

31 Akshay Brahmachari, *Kaumi Ekta Ki Agni Pariksha*, Bharatiya Kaumi Ekta Mandal, Lucknow, 1989, p. 11.

32 Interview with Mahant Bhaskar Das.

33 Interview with Awadh Kishore Jha.

34 Interview with Acharya Satyendra Das.

35 Interview with Mahant Avadhram Das at Jambwant Quila in Ayodhya on 6 October 2010.

36 Ibid.

37 Interview with Awadh Kishore Jha.

Chapter 4

1 The reconstruction of Muhammad Ismael's life and thoughts is based on what the elders of Paharganj Ghosiana – the village which he reached in the intervening night of 22–23 December 1949 after escaping from the Babri Masjid, and where he stayed for the rest of his life – remembered about him and what they said in a series of interviews on 5 October 2010.

2 Interview with Indushekhar Jha.

3 Interview with Mahant Bhaskar Das.

4 Interview with Farooq Ahmad (who was in his late twenties in 1949) in Ayodhya on 4 October 2010. He was a regular visitor to the Babri Masjid before it was taken over by Hindus.

5 Interview with Abdur Rahim, who was around thirty years old in 1949, on 5 October 2010 in Paharganj Ghosiana, Faizabad.

6 Harold A. Gould, *Grassroots Politics in India*, p. 196.

7 Interview with Mahant Bhaskar Das.

8 Ibid.

9 Interview with Indushekhar Jha.

10 Justice Deoki Nandan, 'Sri Ram Janma Bhumi: Historical and Legal Perspective', in Vinay Chandra Mishra (ed.), *Ram Janmabhoomi Babri Masjid*, The Bar Council of India Trust, Delhi, 1991, pp. 8–9.

11 Interview with Mahant Bhaskar Das.

12 Interview with Acharya Satyendra Das.

13 Interview with Indushekhar Jha.

14 Suryanarayana Mishra, *Meri Jeevani*, Brahmadev Printing Press, Ayodhya, 1967, pp. 121, 124, 127, 128, 146.

15 *Virakta*, 10 January 1950, p. 11. The pamphlet mocked secularists, calling them

descendants of Jaichand and Mir Zafar. According to *Prithviraj Raso*, in the Battle of Tarain, when Muhammad Ghori successfully launched an attack on the forces of Delhi, Prithvi Raj Chauhan requested Jaichand to join him in fighting the invader. Jaichand bluntly refused and instead went to the Ghori camp to fight against Chauhan. It is alleged that Raja Jaichand divulged the secrets of Chauhan's war plans to Ghori, leading to Prithvi Raj Chauhan's defeat and the establishment of the first Muslim kingdom in north India. Though this is disputed by many historians, for Hindu communalists, the name has become synonymous with a traitor. Same is the case with Mir Zafar, who, driven by aspirations to become the nawab of Bengal, had entered into a secret pact with the enemy forces of the British. When the battle began, he did not let the Bengal army division under his command to enter the battlefield of Palassey. This considerably weakened Siraj-ud-Daulah's forces, which were then easily slaughtered by the army of the East India Company. Thus, the British won the battle and established their rule in India. For this act, Mir Zafar is also treated as a traitor.

16 Interview with Rajendra Singh.

17 Interview with Awadh Kishore Jha.

18 Ibid.

19 A.G. Noorani (ed.), *The Babri Masjid Question, 1528-2003*, Vol. 1, p. 211.

20 Akshay Brahmachari's 'Memorandum to Lal Bahadur Shastri, the Home Minister of UP', p. 240.

21 Ibid.

22 Ibid., pp. 240–41.

23 Interview with Awadh Kishore Jha.

24 Christophe Jaffrelot, *The Hindu Nationalist Movement and Indian Politics*, p. 93.

25 'Letter from Deputy Commissioner, Faizabad, dated 26 December 1949, to Chief Secretary, Government of UP', in A.G. Noorani (ed.), *The Babri Masjid Question, 1528-2003*, Vol. 1, pp. 212–214.

26 Ibid.

27 Harold A. Gould, *Grassroots Politics in India*, p. 196.

28 'Letter from Deputy Commissioner, Faizabad, dated 27 December 1949, to Chief Secretary, Government of UP', in A.G. Noorani (ed.), *The Babri Masjid Question, 1528-2003*, pp. 215–16.

29 Ibid.

30 S. Gopal (ed.), *Selected Works of Jawaharlal Nehru*, Second Series, Vol. 14, Part 1, p. 443.

31 B.R. Nanda (ed.), *Selected Works of Govind Ballabh Pant*, Vol. 18, 2002, p. 357.

32 S. Gopal (ed.), *Selected Works of Jawaharlal Nehru*, Second Series, Vol. 14, Part 1, p. 443.

33 B.R. Nanda (ed.), *Selected Works of Govind Ballabh Pant*, Vol. 13, 2000, p. 409.

34 Ibid. Vol. 18, pp. 358–59.

35 Ibid., Vol. 13, p. 408.

36 Ibid., pp. 347–48.

37 Ibid., footnote 4, p. 137.

38 S. Gopal (ed.), *Selected Works of Jawaharlal Nehru*, Second Series, Vol. 14, Part 1, pp. 293–94.

39 Ibid., p. 295.

Chapter 5

1 Justice Jeevan Lal Kapur, 'Report of the Commission of Inquiry into Conspiracy to Murder Mahatma Gandhi', Part 1, p. 156, para. 12B.17.

2 *Leader*, 25 December 1949.

3 N.B. Khare, 'Oral History Transcripts', Acc. No. 310, NMML, p. 117.

4 Ibid., p. 119.

5 Hindu Mahasabha Papers, File No. P-126/1950, NMML, p. 453.

6 Ibid., p. 451.

7 *Leader*, 29 December 1949.

8 Hindu Mahasabha Papers, File No. P-126/1950, NMML, p. 391.

9 Justice Deoki Nandan, 'Sri Rama Janma Bhumi: Historical and Legal perspective', in Vinay Chandra Mishra (ed.), *Ram Janmabhoomi Babri Masjid*, p. 10.

10 Hindu Mahasabha Papers, File No. C-185/1950, NMML, pp. 364–66.

11 Ibid., File No. C-187/1950, p. 18.

12 Ibid.

13 Ibid., File No. P-126/1950, p. 399.

14 Ibid., File No. P-125/1949–50, p. 103.

15 Ibid., File No. P-126/1950, p. 317.

16 Ibid., pp. 301–02.

17 Ibid., File No. C-187/1950, p. 43.

18 See Dr N.B. Khare, *My Political Memoirs or Autobiography*, J.R. Joshi, Nagpur, 1960.

19 Interview with Sadhu Saran Mishra Nair's attorney in civil suit against Ranopali Nanaksahi Temple, on 25 December 2010 in Faizabad.

20 *Virakta*, 8 August 1953, p. 1.

21 A.G. Noorani, 'Muslims Wronged', *Frontline*, Vol. 27, No. 21, 09–22 October 2010.

22 *Virakta*, 10 January 1950, p. 8.

23 'The Receiver's Scheme', in A.G. Noorani (ed.), *The Babri Masjid Question, 1528-2003*, Vol. 1, p. 222.

24 'Verbal portion of the FIR filed in the morning of 23 December 1949', in A.G. Noorani (ed.), *The Babri Masjid Question, 1528-2003*, Vol. 1, p. 210.

25 A.G. Noorani (ed.), *The Babri Masjid Question, 1528–2003*, Vol. 1, pp. 224–25.

Chapter 6

1 One standard bigha in the United Provinces (as Uttar Pradesh was called at that time) was equal to 20 biswas or 0.250 hectare or 2,500 square metres.

2 Interview with Advocate Sadhu Saran Mishra.

3 Ibid.

4 Hindu Mahasabha Papers, File No. P-134/1951, pp. 4–5.

5 Ibid.

6 Interview with Advocate Sadhu Saran Mishra.

7 Akshay Brahmachari, *Kaumi Ekta Ki Agni Pariksha*, p. 13.

8 Ibid. p. 14.

9 Interview with Muhammad Ahmad, son of Muhammad Bashir, on 6 October 2010 in Faizabad.

10 Akshay Brahmachari, *Kaumi Ekta Ki Agni Pariksha*, pp. 8–9.

11 Dr Radheshyam Shukla, *Shriram Janmabhoomi*, pp. 44, 45.

12 Ibid., p. 45.

13 Akshay Brahmachari, *Kaumi Ekta Ki Agni Pariksha*, pp. 9–11.

14 Ibid., pp. 18–19.

15 Ibid., p. 19.

16 Ibid., pp. 20–22.

17 S. Gopal (ed.), *Selected Works of Jawaharlal Nehru*, Second Series, Vol. 14, Part 2, pp. 296–97.

18 Akshay Brahmachari, *Kaumi Ekta Ki Agni Pariksha*, p. 23.

19 Ibid., pp. 6–7.

20 Akshay Brahmachari, *Kaumi Ekta Ki Agni Pariksha*, pp. 24–27.

21 B.R. Nanda, *Selected Works of Govind Ballabh Pant*, Vol. 13, 2000, pp. 134–36.

22 Cited by K.G. Mashruwala, *Harijan*, 30 September 1950.

23 Ibid.

24 Christophe Jaffrelot, *The Hindu Nationalist Movement and Indian Politics*, p. 81.

25 *Times of India*, 17 August 1950, p. 6.

26 Donald Eugene Smith, *India as a Secular State*, p. 480.

27 V.G. Deshpande, *Why Hindu Rashtra?*, Akhil Bharat Hindu Mahasabha, New Delhi, 1949, p. 1.

28 G. Parthasarthi (ed.), *Letters to Chief Ministers*, Vol. 2, p. 83.

29 Mushirul Hasan, 'Adjustment and Accommodation: Indian Muslims after Partition', in K.N. Panikkar (ed.), *Communalism in India*, Manohar Publications, New Delhi, 1991, p. 66.

30 *National Herald*, 15 June 1948, p. 7.

31 S. Gopal, *Jawaharlal Nehru: A Biography*, Vol. 2: 1947-1956, p. 93.

32 Durga Das (ed.), *Sardar Patel's Correspondence: 1945-1950*, Vol. 10, 1974, pp. 220–21.

33 In 1949, this argument was developed in part by A.G. Kher, a minister of the United Provinces close to Patel. See W. Andersen and S.D. Damle, *The Brotherhood in Saffron: The Rashtriya Swayamsevak Sangh and Hindu Revivalism*, Vistaar Publications, New Delhi, 1987, p. 55.

34 Durga Das (ed.), *Sardar Patel's Correspondence: 1945–1950*, Vol. 10, pp. 222–23.

35 Hindu Mahasabha Papers, File No. C-184 (Tej Bahadur Kaul, 'Tandon and Hindus'), NMML, New Delhi.

36 The *Hitavada*, 4 September 1950, p. 1.

37 *Organiser*, 11 September 1950, p. 3.

38 The *Statesman*, 23 September 1950, p.5.

39 *New York Times*, 22 September 1950.

40 Harold A. Gould, *Grassroots Politics in India*, p. 159.

41 Dr Radheyshyam Shukla, *Shriram Janmabhoomi*, pp. 49–52.

Appendix I

1 Ghurye, G.S., *Indian Sadhus*, Popular Prakashan, Bombay, 1953, p. 165.

2 Clark, Mathew, *The Dashanami Sanyasis*, Brill, Lieden-Boston, 2006, pp. 57–59.

3 Ghurye, G.S., *Indian Sadhus*, p. 177.

4 Ibid., pp. 177–78.

5 Ibid., pp. 178–79.

Appendix II

1 G. Parthasarathi (ed.), *Letters to Chief Ministers*, Vol. 1, pp. 56–57.

2 V.D. Shankar (ed.), *Sardar Patel's Select Correspondence, 1945–1950*, Ahmedabad: Navajivan Publishing House, 1976, p. 282 (letter dated 26 February 1948).

3 Ibid., p. 283 (letter dated 27 February 1948.

4 G. Parthasarathi (ed.), *Letters to Chief Ministers*, Vol. 1, 1947–1949.

Glossary

Aarti – A Hindu ritual that pays obeisance to God by offering light
Advaita – Absolute non-dualism
Akhara – A militant ascetic camp, a band of militant sadhus, or a wrestling pit
Akhand – Uninterrupted; undivided
Akhand Kirtan – Uninterrupted recitation and chanting of devotional songs
Akharamal Vairagi – A Ramanandi vairagi belonging to an akhara
Ani – A short form of the Sanskrit word anika, meaning army; the term is used for the organized band of Ramanandi naga vairagis
Asan – The permanent seat of residence and meditation of an ascetic
Astradhari – A militant ascetic or naga
Azan – Islamic call to prayer
Baithak – Seat
Bhakti – Devotion
Bhandara – Community feast organized by religious establishments
Bhog – Offering to deity
Bigha – A traditional unit of measurement of land
Brahmin – The Hindu priestly caste and the top rung of the caste pyramid
Chamatkari: Literally meaning miraculous, but means manipulative in the context
Dakshina – Monetary offering for religious work

Darshan – Viewing of a deity
Dargah – Sufi shrine
Dashnami – A group of ten akharas said to have been founded by Shankaracharya
Dhuni – Sacred fire
Diksha – A formal ritual initiation by a guru
Faqir – A Muslim renunciant
Gaddi-Nashin – Occupant of the seat of power at Hanumangarhi
Garbhagriha – Sanctum sanctorum
Gaushala – Cowshed
Ghanta-ghariyal – Bell which is struck as part of religious ritual
Ghat – Riverfront, usually reached by steps built for the benefit of bathers
Ghee – Clarified butter
Grihastha – Householder
Guru – Religious preceptor
Hanuman Janmotsava – Celebration of the day marking the birth of Lord Hanuman
Havan Kund – Sacred pit for fire
Hindu Rashtra – Hindu nation
Jamat – An itinerant group of ascetics
Janmasthan – Place of birth
Jhula – The swing festival that celebrates the childhood of a divinity
Kanphata – Split-ear
Kar Seva – Voluntary services for a religious cause
Kar Sevak – Someone who offers voluntary services for a religious cause
Kartik – A month in the Hindu lunar calender corresponding with October/November
Kartik Mela – Great bathig fair held in the Hindu lunar month of Kartik
Kartik Purnima – Last day of the Hindu lunar month of Kartik
Khateeb – Muslim cleric who delivers sermon in a mosque
Kirtan – Recitation of religious songs
Kumbha Mela – Mass Hindu bathing festival celebrated alternatively every three years in Haridwar, Allahabad, Nasik and Ujjain; each centre hosts it every twelfth year
Kurta – A long shirt worn over a lungi or trousers
Lakshana – Sign
Lathi – Walking staff

Lila – Religious mystery play
Mahant – Abbot
Mala-jhola – A cotton bag containing a rosary
Mantra – Sacred formula
Matha – Religious establishment
Mazar – Grave
Mela – Fair
Muezzin – The caretaker of a mosque
Mugdha – Unmarried girl
Mughara – Canopy
Naga – Militant ascetic
Nathpanth – A sect of Shaiva ascetics, founded by Gorakhnath
Nazul land – Government land
Namaz – Prayer
Namazi – One who goes to offer namaz
Navah Paath – Nine-day recitation of verses from *Ramcharitmanas* which is a treatise by Tulsidas
Panchan –The all-powerful group of representatives of naga vairagis of Hanumangarhi
Panchan-patti – The governing body of representatives of a section of Nirvani Akhara
Pathshala – School, usually imparting education in Sanskrit
Patti – Section; usually refers to subgroups of naga residents of Hanumangarhi
Pir – A Muslim saint
Puja – Worship
Pujan Shila – Anointed bricks
Ramachabutara – The elevated platform outside the inner courtyard of the Babri Masjid
Ramajanmabhoomi – The place in Ayodhya where Lord Rama is believed to have been born
Ramakatha – Story of Lord Rama recited by devout Hindus
Rama Lalla – Infant Rama
Rama Naumi – Celebration of Rama's birthday
Rama Vivah – The marriage of Lord Rama with Goddess Sita
Ramnami – Saffron cloth that has the name of Lord Rama printed all over
Rasik/Sakhi – An esoteric wing of Ramanandi ascetics who consider

themselves female friends of Goddess Sita and who act as the spectators of the marital joy of Rama and Sita

Rath Yatra – Chariot procession

Ravana – The demon king who appears as the antagonistic character in the legend of Lord Rama

Sadhana – Spritual practice

Sadhu – Hindu ascetic

Sampradaya – Order or sect

Sankh – Conch shell used for Hindu religious purposes

Sanyasi – Renunciant; a term used for Shaiva ascetic

Satyagraha – Insistence on Truth; Gandhi's term for passive resistance or militant non-violence

Ser-siddha – Uncooked food items supplied to every naga resident by the management of Hanumangarhi on a weekly basis

Shastradhari – A scholastic monk of a Hindu sect

Shikha/Chhot – A tuft of hair worn by devout Hindus

Shri-Mahant – Chief abbot

Shilanyas – Laying the foundation

Siddhi – Psychic power attained through tapas

Simhastha Fair – Great bathing festival or Kumbh of Ujjain celebrated in a cycle of twelve years when Jupiter enters the Leo sign of the zodiac, known as Simha Rashi

Singhasan – Throne; in this case, the throne carrying the idol of Rama Lalla

Singhdwar – Outer and main gate

Tapas – Heating of the body by ascetic exercise in order to obtain power

Tripunda – Trident mark on forehead

Tulsi – Holy basil, considered a symbol of purity among Hindus

Uddharak – Liberator

Vairagi – Detached or dispassionate; a term used for a Ramanandi ascetic

Vigyapti – Communiqué

Viman – Mythical transporter of soul to heavenly realm; a flying vehicle

Vishal – Grand

Yajna – A Hindu religious ceremony often related to sacrifice

Yogi – Ascetic

Yugal Sarkar – The royal couple of Rama and Sita

Zamindar – Landlord

Bibliography

Newspapers and Journals

Aaj, 10 December 1949, 22 December 1949.
Frontline, Vol. 27, No. 21, 09–22 October, 2010.
Harijan, 19 August 1950, 30 September 1950.
Hindu Sabha Varta, Sri Ram Janmabhoomi Visheshank, 28 October 1991.
Hindustan Times, 15 November 1947.
Hitavada, 3 February 1948, 4 February 1948, 17 February 1948, 10 August 1948, 4 September 1950.
Leader, 25 December 1949, 29 December 1949.
National Herald, 15 June 1948, 16 June 1948, 19 June 1948.
New York Times, 22 September 1950, 22 December 1991.
Organiser, 11 September 1950.
Statesman, 13 June 1950, 23 September 1950.
The Pioneer (Lucknow), 23 December 1949.
Times of India, 17 August 1950.
Virakta, 10 January 1950, 8 August 1953.

Archival Materials and Reports

Hindu Mahasabha Papers, File Nos: C-170, C-171, 120(I), P-125, P-126, C-185, C-187, P-134, C-184, Nehru Memorial Museum and Library, New Delhi.

Kapur, Justice Jeevan Lal 'Report of the Commission of Inquiry into Conspiracy to Murder Mahatma Gandhi', two vols, New Delhi: Government of India, 1969.

N.B. Khare Papers, File No. 164, National Archives of India.

N.B. Khare, Oral History Transcripts, Acc. No. 310, Nehru Memorial Museum and Library, New Delhi.

Niyamavali Hanumangarhi, Ayodhya: Varma Printing Press, 1963.

'White Paper on Ayodhya', New Delhi: Government of India, February 1993.

Books

Andersen, W. and S.D.Damle, *The Brotherhood in Saffron: The Rashtriya Swayamsevak Sangh and Hindu Revivalism*, New Delhi: Vistaar Publications, 1987.

Anderson, B., *Imagined Communities: Reflections on the Origin and Spread of Nationalism*, London: Verso, 1983.

Bakker, H.T., *Ayodhya: The History of Ayodhya from the 17th Century BC to the Middle of the 18th Century*, Groningen: Egbert Forsten, 1986.

Barnett, R.B., *North India between Empires: Awadh, the Mughals and the British, 1720–1801*, Berkeley: University of California Press, 1980.

Baxter, C., *A Biography of an Indian Political Party – Jana Sangha*, Bombay: Oxford University Press, 1971.

Bayly, C.A., 'From Ritual to Ceremony: Death Ritual and Society in Hindu North India since 1600', in J. Whaley (ed.), *Mirrors of Mortality*, London: Europa Publications, 1981.

Bhardwaj, S.M., *Hindu Places of Pilgrimage in India*, Berkeley: University of California Press, 1983.

Bhatnagar, G.D., *Awadh under Wajid Ali Khan*, Benaras: Bharatiya Vidya Prakashan, 1968.

Brahmachari, Akshay, *Kaumi Ekta Ki Agni Pariksha*, Lucknow: Bharatiya Kaumi Ekta Mandal, 1989.

Brass, P., *Language, Religion and Politics in North India*, Cambridge, Massachusetts: Cambridge University Press, 1974.

Briggs, G.W., *Gorakhnath and the Kanphata Yogis*, Calcutta: YMCA Publishing House, 1938.

Carnegy, P., *Historical Sketch of Tahsil Fyzabad, Zillah Fyzabad*, Lucknow: Oudh Government Press, 1870.

Clark, Mathew, *The Dashanami Sanyasis*, Brill, Lieden-Boston, 2006.

Das, Durga (ed.), *Sardar Patel's Correspondence, 1945–1950*, Ahmedabad: Navajivan Publishing House, Ahmedabad, 1973.

Deshpande, V.G., *Why Hindu Rashtra?*, New Delhi: Akhil Bharat Hindu Mahasabha, 1949.

Engineer, Asgar Ali (ed.), *Babri Masjid–Ramjanma Bhoomi Controversy*, Delhi: Ajanta Publications, 1990.

Gazetteer of India, *Uttar Pradesh: Faizabad*, Allahabad: Government Press, 1960.

Ghurye, G.S., *Indian Sadhus*, Bombay: Popular Prakashan, 1953.

Gonda, J., *Visnuism and Sivaism: A Comparison*, London: Athlone Press, 1970.

Gopal, Sarvepalli, *Jawaharlal Nehru: A Biography*, Vol. 2, 1947–1956, Delhi: Oxford University Press, 1979.

Gopal, S. (ed.), *Selected Works of Jawaharlal Nehru*, Second Series, Vol. 14, New Delhi: JNMF, 1992.

Gopal, Sarvepalli (ed.). *Anatomy of a Confrontation – The Babri Masjid Ramjanmabhumi Issue*, New Delhi: Penguin Books India Pvt. Ltd, 1991.

Gould, Harold A., *Grassroots Politics in India – A Centuty of Political Evolution in Faizabad District*, New Delhi, Bombay and Calcutta: Oxford and IBH Publishing Co. Pvt. Ltd, 1994.

Gould, H., 'Religion and Politics in a U.P. Constituency', in Donald Eugene Smith (ed.), *South Asian Politics and Religion*, Princeton: Princeton University Press, 1966.

Graham, B., *Hindu Nationalism and Indian Politics: The Origins and Development of the Bharatiya Jana Sangh*, Cambridge, Massachusetts: Cambridge University Press, 1990.

Gross, Robert Lewis, *The Sadhus of India*, Jaipur and New Delhi: Rawat Publications, 1992.

Gupta, N.L., *Nehru on Communalism*, New Delhi: Sampradayikta Virodhi Committee, 1965.

Jaffrelot, Christophe, *The Hindu Nationalist Movement and Indian Politics, 1925 to the 1990s*, London: Hurst & Company, 1993.

Keer, Dhananjay, *Savarkar and His Times*, Bombay: A.V. Keer, 1950.

Khare, Dr N.B., *My Political Memoirs or Autobiography*, Nagpur: J.R. Joshi, 1960.

Kulkarni, V.B., *K.M. Munshi*, New Delhi: Government of India, 1983.

Mishra, Suryanarayana, *Meri Jeevani*, Ayodhya: Brahmadev Printing Press, 1967.

Mishra, Vinay Chandra (ed.), *Ram Janmabhoomi Babri Masjid*, Delhi: The Bar Council of India Trust, 1991.

Munshi, K.M., *Our Greatest Need and Other Addresses*, Bombay: Bharatiya Vidya Bhawan, 1953.

Nanda, B.R. (ed.), *Selected Works of Govind Ballabh Pant*, Vols 12 (1999), 13 (2000), 18 (2002), New Delhi, Oxford University Press.

Nehru, Jawaharlal, *Independence and After*, New York: John Day Company, 1948.

Neville, H.R., *Faizabad District Gazetteer*, Allahabad: Government Press, 1905.

Noorani, A.G. (ed.), *The Babri Masjid Question, 1528-2003*, 2 vols., New Delhi: Tulika Books, 2003.

Panikkar, K.N. (ed.), *Communalism in India*, New Delhi: Manohar Publications, 1991.

Parthasarathi, G. (ed.), *Letters to Chief Ministers, 1947-49*, New Delhi: Government of India, 1985.

Payne, Robert, *The Life and Death of Mahatma Gandhi*, Delhi: Rupa & Co., 1997.

Prasad, Rajendra, *Devastated Bihar*, Patna: Bihar Central Relief Committee, 1934.

Savarkar, V.D., *Hindutva: Who is a Hindu?*, Bombay: S.S. Savarkar, 1969.

Shankar, V.D., *Sardar Patel's Select Correspondence, 1945–1950*, Ahmedabad: Navajivan Publishing House, 1976.

Sharad, Ramgopal Pandey, *Shree Ramjanmabhoomi Ka Rakta Ranjit Itihaas*, Ayodhya: Dwarika Prasad Shivgovind Pustakalaya, n.d.

Shukla, Dr Radheshyam, *Shriram Janmabhoomi*, Ayodhya: Madhu Prakashan, 1986.

Singh, Jagdev, *Gonda: Ateet Tathaa Vartamaan*, Gonda: Alok Prakashan, 1975.

Singh, Parmanand, *Legal History of the Ayodhya Litigation*, Indian Bar Review, Vol. 18 (2), New Delhi: The Bar Council of India Trust, 1991.

Sinha, B.P., *Rambhakti Mein Rasik Sampradaya*, Balrampur: Avadh Sahitya Mandir, 1957.

Smith, Donald Eugene, *India as a Secular State*, London and Bombay: Oxford University Press, 1963.

Rau, M. Chalapathi, *Govind Ballabh Pant: His Life and Times*, New Delhi: Allied Publishers Pvt. Ltd, 1981.

van der Veer, Peter, *Gods on Earth: The Management of Religious Experiences and Identity in a North Indian Pilgrimage Centre*, Delhi: Oxford University Press, 1989.

van der Veer, Peter. 'Aydodhya and Somnath: Eternal Shrines, Contested Histories', *Social Research*, Vol. 59, No.1, Spring 1992.

Williams, R.B., *A New Face of Hinduism*, Cambridge, Massachusetts: Cambridge University Press, 1984.

Index

Acknowledgements

WE COULD NOT POSSIBLY have written this book without the help of the many people who, whether openly or in confidence, gave us – or facilitated in gaining for us – access to the information it contains. In addition, our sincere thanks to late Ramkrishna Mani Tripathi, Dinesh Singh, Krishna Pratap Singh, Gopal Krishna Varma, Anil Kumar Singh, Nitin Mishra, Sanjay Mishra, Deen Dayal Vishwakarma, Swami Haridayal Mishra, Farooq Ahmad, Khaliq Ahmad Khan, Muhammad Ahmad, Guru Basant Singh, Taranjit Lal Varma, Meera Behn, Dr Abid Suhail, Muhammad Masood, K.C. Mishra, Siddharth Kalhansa, Manoj Singh, Baikuntha Jha, Manoj Kumar Jha, Raman Jha, Pramod Pandit Joshi, Dinesh Chandra Tyagi, Prof. D.N. Jha, Abid Shah, Hartosh Singh Bal, Bhashyam Kasturi, Ashutosh Jha, Rajesh Kumar, Ishan Tankha, Ashish Sharma, Apoorva Guptay, Amrendra Jha, Anil Rajimwale, N. Chidambaram and our editors Ajitha G.S. and Prema Govindan.

Above all, we wish to express our gratitude to the countless friends who helped and encouraged us whenever we stumbled in our effort to piece together this missing link of modern Indian history.